Say it
Right in
SPANISH

Third Edition

Easily Pronounced Language Systems

Clyde Peters, Author

New York   Chicago   San Francisco   Athens   London   Madrid
Mexico City   Milan   New Delhi   Singapore   Sydney   Toronto

1 2 3 4 5 6 7 8 9   LCR   23 22 21 20 19 18

ISBN   978-1-260-11630-4
MHID   1-260-11630-1

e-ISBN   978-1-260-11631-1
e-MHID   1-260-11631-X

Library of Congress Cataloging-in-Publication Data

Say it right in Spanish / Easily Pronounced Language Systems — 2nd ed.
        p.   cm. — (Say it right)
     Includes index.
     Text in English and Spanish.
     ISBN 978-0-07-176691-3 (alk. paper)
     1. Spanish language—Pronunciation by foreign speakers.   2. Spanish language—Spoken Spanish.   3. Spanish language—Conversation and phrase books—English.   I. Easily Pronounced Language Systems.   II. Clyde E. Peters, Author.
PC4137.S28   2011
468.3'421—dc22   2011011058

Clyde Peters, author
Luc Nisset, illustrations
Betty Chapman, EPLS contributor, www.isayitright.com
Priscilla Leal Bailey, senior series editor
Francisco J. Madrigal, Spanish language consultant

Also available:
Say It Right in Chinese, Second Edition
Say It Right in French, Third Edition
Say It Right in Italian, Third Edition

McGraw-Hill Education Language Lab App

Streaming audio recordings (requiring Internet connection) of 500 words and phrases from this book are available to help improve your pronunciation. Go to www.mhlanguagelab.com to access the online version of this application, or search the iTunes or Google Play app stores for the free mobile version of the app.

CONTENTS

INTRODUCTION

The SAY IT RIGHT FOREIGN
LANGUAGE PHRASE BOOK
SERIES has been developed
with the conviction that
learning to speak a foreign
language should be fun and easy!

All SAY IT RIGHT phrase books feature the EPLS
Vowel Symbol System, a revolutionary phonetic
system that stresses consistency, clarity, and
above all, simplicity!

Since this unique phonetic system is used in all
SAY IT RIGHT phrase books, you only have to
learn the VOWEL SYMBOL SYSTEM ONCE!

The SAY IT RIGHT series uses the easiest phrases
possible for English speakers to pronounce and
is designed to reflect how foreign languages are
used by native speakers.

You will be amazed at how confidence in your
pronunciation leads to an eagerness to talk to
other people in their own language.

Whether you want to learn a new language for
travel, education, business, study, or personal
enrichment, SAY IT RIGHT phrase books offer a
simple and effective method of pronunciation and
communication.

PRONUNCIATION GUIDE

Most English speakers are familiar with the Spanish word **Taco**. This is how the correct pronunciation is represented in the EPLS Vowel Symbol System.

All Spanish vowel sounds are assigned a specific non-changing symbol. When these symbols are used in conjunction with consonants and read normally, pronunciation of even the most difficult foreign word becomes incredibly EASY!

On the following page are all the EPLS Vowel Symbols used in this book. They are EASY to LEARN since their sounds are familiar. Beneath each symbol are three English words which contain the sound of the symbol.

Practice pronouncing the words under each symbol until you mentally associate the correct vowel sound with the correct symbol. Most symbols are pronounced the way they look!

THE SAME BASIC SYMBOLS ARE USED IN ALL SAY IT RIGHT PHRASE BOOKS!

EPLS VOWEL SYMBOL SYSTEM

Ⓐ
Ace
Bake
Safe

ⒺⒺ
See
Feet
Meet

Ⓘ
Ice
Kite
Pie

Ⓞ
Oak
Cold
Sold

ⓄⓄ
Cool
Pool
Too

ⓔ̆
Men
Red
Bed

ⓐⓗ
Calm
Mom
Hot

ⓞⓨ
Toy
Boy
Joy

ⓞⓦ
Cow
How
Now

EPLS CONSONANTS

Consonants are letters like **T**, **D**, and **K**. They are easy to recognize and their pronunciation seldom changes. The following EPLS pronunciation guide letters represent some unique Spanish consonant sounds.

℞	Represents a rolled **r** sound.
℞	Represents a strongly rolled **r** sound.
V	Represents the Spanish letter **v** and is pronounced like the **v** in **v**ine but very softly. Depending on your location you will often hear the Spanish **v** pronounced like the **b** in **b**oy.
B	Represents the Spanish letter **b** and sounds like the **b** in **b**oy. Sometimes, the Spanish **b** is pronounced so softly that the lips barely touch.
D	Represents the Spanish letter **d** and sounds like the **d** in **d**ay. Sometimes, the Spanish **d** is pronounced softly and sounds like **th** in the English words **th**ey or **th**en.
<u>TH</u>	These EPLS letters are underlined to remind you that the letters are voiced and sound like the **th** in the words e**th**ernet or **th**ink. You will find this pronunciation common in Spain.

PRONUNCIATION TIPS

- Each pronunciation guide word is broken into syllables. Read each word slowly, one syllable at a time, increasing speed as you become more familiar with the system.

- In Spanish it is important to emphasize certain syllables. This mark (´) over the syllable reminds you to stress that syllable.

- It is estimated that nearly 300 million people now speak Spanish around the world. Don't be surprised to hear variations in the meanings and pronunciation of some Spanish words. **To perfect your Spanish accent you must listen closely to Spanish speakers and adjust your speech accordingly.**

- The pronunciation and word choices in this book were chosen for their simplicity and effectiveness.

- In northern Spain, **z** before any letter and **c** before **e** or **i** are pronounced like the **th** in **th**ink. In southern Spain and most of Latin America, **z** by itself and **c** before **e** or **i** sound like an **s**. In this phrase book the **s** sound is used for **z** and **c** because of its wider usage throughout the Spanish-speaking world.

- **PFV** is an abbreviation for **por favor** which means "please" in Spanish. You will see it used throughout the book.

ICONS USED IN
THIS BOOK

KEY WORDS

You will find this icon at the beginning of chapters indicating key words relating to chapter content. These are important words to become familiar with.

PHRASEMAKER

The Phrasemaker icon provides the traveler with a choice of phrases that allows the user to make his or her own sentences.

Say It
Right in
SPANISH

ESSENTIAL WORDS AND PHRASES

Here are some basic words and phrases that will help you express your needs and feelings in **Spanish**.

Hello

Hola

OH-Lah

How are you?

¿Cómo está?

KOH-MOH eS-Tah

Fine / Very well

Muy bien

MWEE BEE-eN

And you?

¿Y usted?

EE ooS-TeD

Good-bye.

Adiós

ah-DEE-OHS

Good morning

Buenos días

BWĕ'-NOS DĒĒ'-ahS

Good evening / Good afternoon

Buenas tardes

BWĕ'-NahS TahŔ-DĕS

Good night

Buenas noches

BWĕ'-NahS NO'-CHĕS

Mr.

Señor

SĕN-YOŔ

Mrs.

Señora

SĕN-YO'-Rah

Miss

Señorita

SĕN-YO-RĒĒ'-Tah

Yes

Sí

SEE

No

No

NO

Please

Por favor

POB Fah-VOB

Abbreviated PFV throughout the book

Thank you

Gracias

GBah-SEE-ahS

Excuse me

Perdón   Con permiso

PEB-DON   KON PEB-MEE-SO

I'm sorry

Lo siento   Perdón

LO SEE-eN-TO   PEB-DON

I am a tourist.

Soy turista.

S⓪y T⓪⓪-Rᴇᴇ-S-Tₐₕ

I do not speak Spanish.

No hablo español.

N⓪ ₐₕ-BL⓪ ᴇS-PₐₕN-Y⓪L

I speak a little Spanish.

Hablo un poco de español.

ₐₕ-BL⓪ ⓸N P⓪-K⓪ Dᴇ
ᴇS-PₐₕN-Y⓪L

Do you understand English?

¿Entiende inglés?

ᴇN-Tᴇᴇ-ᴇN-Dᴇ ᴇᴇN-GLᴇS

I don't understand!

¡No entiendo!

N⓪ ᴇN-Tᴇᴇ-ᴇN-D⓪

Please repeat.

Repita, por favor.

Rᴇ-Pᴇᴇ-Tₐₕ P⓪R Fₐₕ-V⓪R

More slowly, please.

Más despacio, por favor.

MₐₕS DᴇS-Pₐₕ-Sᴇᴇ-⓪ PFV

FEELINGS

I want…
Quiero…
KEE-é-RO

I have…
Tengo…
TéN-GO…

I know.
Yo sé.
YO Sé

I don't know.
No sé.
NO Sé

I like it.
Me gusta.
Mé GOOS-Tah

I don't like it.
No me gusta.
NO Mé GOOS-Tah

I'm lost.

Estoy perdido. (male)   Estoy perdida. (female)

ⓔS-Tⓞⓨ́ Pⓔ́R-DⒺⒺ́-Dⓞ (ⓐⓗ)

I'm in a hurry.

Tengo prisa.

Tⓔ́N-Gⓞ PRⒺⒺ́-Sⓐⓗ

I'm tired.

Estoy cansado. (male) Estoy cansada. (female)

ⓔ́S-Tⓞⓨ́ KⓐⓗN-Sⓐⓗ́-Dⓞ (ⓐⓗ)

I'm ill.

Estoy enfermo. (male) Estoy enferma. (female)

ⓔ́S-Tⓞⓨ́ ⓔN-Fⓔ́R-Mⓞ (ⓐⓗ)

I'm hungry.

Tengo hambre.

Tⓔ́N-Gⓞ ⓐⓗ́M-BRⓔ

I'm thirsty.

Tengo sed.

Tⓔ́N-Gⓞ Sⓔ́D

I'm angry.

Estoy enojado. (male)   Estoy enojada. (female)

ⓔ́S-Tⓞⓨ́ ⓔN-ⓞ-Hⓐⓗ́-Dⓞ (ⓐⓗ)

EPLS displays the feminine ending in parenthesis.

INTRODUCTIONS

My name is…

Me llamo…

Mĕ Yah-MO…

What's your name?

¿Cómo se llama usted?

KO-MO Sĕ Yah-Mah ooS-TĕD

Where are you from?

¿De dónde es usted?

Dĕ DON-Dĕ ĕS ooS-TĕD

Do you live here?

¿Vive usted aquí?

VEE-Vĕ ooS-TĕD ah-KEE

I just arrived.

Acabo de llegar.

ah-Kah-BO Dĕ Yĕ-GahR

What hotel are you [staying] at?

¿En qué hotel está usted?

ĕN Kĕ O-TĕL ĕS-Tah ooS-TĕD

I'm at the…hotel.

Estoy en el hotel…

ⓔS-Tⓞⓨ́ ⓔN ⓔL ⓞ-Tⓔ́L…

It was nice to meet you.

Mucho gusto.

Mⓞⓞ́-CHⓞ Gⓞⓞ́S-Tⓞ

G is pronounced like the **g** in **g**o.

See you later.

Hasta luego.

ⓐⓗ́S-Tⓐⓗ Lⓞⓞ-Ⓐ́-Gⓞ

See you next time.

Hasta la vista.

ⓐⓗ́S-Tⓐⓗ Lⓐⓗ VⒺⒺ́-STⓤⓗ

Good luck!

¡Buena suerte!

BWⓔ́-Nⓐⓗ SWⓔ́Ᵽ-Tⓔ

You will notice that in Spanish spelling, the letter **e** is sometimes pronounced like the **e** in r**e**d and sometimes like the **a** in c**a**ke. This will vary from region to region and will not affect the understanding of the word.

THE BIG QUESTIONS

Who?

¿Quién?

KEE-ĕN

Who is it?

¿Quién es?

KEE-ĕN ĕS

What?

¿Qué?   ¿Cómo?

Kĕ   KŌ-MŌ

Use **¿cómo?** if you didn't hear well or want something repeated.

What's that?

¿Qué es eso?

Kĕ ĕS ĕ-SŌ

When?

¿Cuándo?

KWahN-DŌ

Where?

¿Dónde?

DŌN-Dĕ

Where is…?

¿Dónde está…?

DÓN-Dē ēS-Tah…

Which?

¿Cuál?

KWahL

Why?

¿Por qué?

POR Kē

How?

¿Cómo?

KÓ-MO

How much? (does it cost)

¿Cuánto?

KWahN-TO

KW sounds like the **qu** in **qu**it.

How long?

¿Cuánto tiempo?

KWahN-TO TEE-ēM-PO

ASKING FOR THINGS

The following phrases are valuable for directions, food, help, etc.

I would like...

Quisiera...

K︎EE-S︎EE-︎ē-R︎ah...

I need...

Necesito...

N︎ē-S︎ē-S︎EE-T︎O...

Can you...

Puede usted...

PW︎ē-D︎ē ︎OOS-T︎ē︎D...

When asking for things be sure to say <u>please</u> and <u>thank you</u>.

Please	**Thank you**
Por Favor	Gracias
P︎OR F︎ah-V︎OR	GR︎ah-S︎EE-︎ah S

PHRASEMAKER

Combine **I would like** with the
following phrases, and you will
have an effective way to ask for things.

I would like…

Quisiera…

KEE-SEE-ĕ́-Rah…

▸ **more coffee**

más café

Mahs Kah-Fĕ́

▸ **some water**

agua

ah́-GWah

▸ **some ice**

hielo

Yĕ́-Lo

▸ **the menu**

la carta

Lah Kah́R-Tah

PHRASEMAKER

Here are a few sentences you can use when you feel the urge to say **I need**… or **Can you**…?

I need…

Necesito… por favor.

N℮-S℮-SEE-T◎… PFV

▶ **help**

ayuda

ah-Yoo-Dah

▶ **directions**

direcciones

DEE-R℮K-SEE-O-N℮S

▶ **more money**

más dinero

Mah S DEE-N℮-R◎

▶ **change**

cambio

Kah M-BEE-◎

▶ **a lawyer**

un abogado

ooN ah-B◎-Gah-D◎

PHRASEMAKER

Can you...

¿Puede usted... por favor?

PW**ⓔ**-D**ⓔ** **⓪⓪**S-T**ⓔ**D... PFV

▸ **help me?**

ayudarme?

ⓐⓗ-Y**⓪⓪**-D**ⓐⓗ**B-M**ⓔ**

▸ **show me?**

enseñarme?

ⓔN-S**ⓔ**N-Y**ⓐⓗ**B-M**ⓔ**

▸ **give me...?**

darme...?

D**ⓐⓗ**B-M**ⓔ**...

▸ **tell me...?**

decirme...?

D**ⓔ**-S**ⓔⓔ**B-M**ⓔ**

▸ **take me to...?**

llevarme al...?

Y**ⓔ**-V**ⓐⓗ**B-M**ⓔ** **ⓐⓗ**L...

ASKING THE WAY

No matter how independent you are, sooner or later you'll probably have to ask for directions.

Where is…?

¿Dónde está…?

DON-De̅ e̅S-Tah…

Is it near?

¿Está cerca?

e̅S-Tah SeR-Kah

Is it far?

¿Está lejos?

e̅S-Tah Le̅-HOS

I'm looking for…

Estoy buscando...

e̅S-Toy BooS-Kahn-DO…

I'm lost! (male)

¡Estoy perdido!

e̅S-Toy PeR-Dee̅-DO

I'm lost! (female)

Estoy perdida!

e̅S-Toy PeR-Dee̅-Dah

PHRASEMAKER

Where is...

¿Dónde está...

DON-De eS-Tah...

▶ **the restroom?**

el baño?

eL Bahn-Yo

▶ **the telephone?**

el teléfono?

eL Te-Le-Fo-No

▶ **the beach?**

la playa?

Lah PLah-Yah

▶ **the hotel...?**

el hotel...?

eL o-TeL...

▶ **the train for...?**

el tren para...?

eL TReN Pah-Bah...

TIME

What time is it?

¿Qué hora es?

Kẽ   Ō-Rah   ẽS

Morning

La mañana

Lah   MahN-Yah́-Nah

Noon

El mediodía

ẽL   Mẽ-DEE-Ō-DEÉ-ah

Night

La noche

Lah   NṒ-CHẽ

Today

Hoy

oy

In Spanish spelling the **h** is always silent.

Tomorrow

Mañana

MahN-Yah́-Nah

This week

Esta semana

ĕS-Tah Sĕ-Mah-Nah

This month

Este mes

ĕS-Tĕ Mĕs

This year

Este año

ĕS-Tĕ ahN-YO

Now

Ahora

ah-O-Rah

Soon

Pronto

PRON-TO

Later

Más tarde

MahS TahR-Dĕ

Never

Nunca

NooN-Kah

WHO IS IT?

I
Yo
Y◎

You (Formal)	**You** (Informal)
Usted	Tú
◎S-Tℰ́D	T◎
Use this form of **you** with people you don't know well	Use this form of **you** with people you know well

---

He	**She**
El	Ella
ℰ́L	ℰ́-Yah

We

Nosotros	Nosotras
N◎-S◎́-TR◎S	N◎-S◎́-TRahS
Use this form for males only or males and females.	Use this form for females only.

They

Ellos	Ellas
ℰ́-Y◎S	ℰ́-YahS
A group of men only or a group of men and woman.	A group of women only.

THE, A (AN), AND SOME

To use the correct form of **The**, **A** (**An**), or **Some**, you must know if the Spanish word is masculine or feminine. Often you will have to guess! If you make a mistake, you will still be understood.

The

La

L@h

The before a singular feminine noun:
(La) girl is pretty.

Las

L@hS

The before a plural feminine noun:
(Las) girls are pretty.

El

@L

The before a singular masculine noun:
(El) man is handsome.

Los

L@S

The before a plural masculine noun:
(Los) men are handsome.

A, An

Un

@N

A or **an** before a singular masculine noun:
He is (un) man.

Una

@-N@h

A or **an** before a singular feminine noun:
She is (una) woman.

Some

Unos

@-N@S

Some before plural masculine nouns:
(Unos) men

Unas

@-N@hS

Some before plural feminine nouns:
(Unas) women

USEFUL OPPOSITES

Near	**Far**
Cerca	Lejos
SĔR-Kah	LĔ-HOS
Here	**There**
Aquí	Ahí
ah-KEE	ah-EE
Left (direction)	**Right** (direction)
Izquierda	Derecha
EES-KĔR-Dah	DĔ-RĔ-CHah
A little	**A lot**
Un poquito	Mucho
OON PO-KEE-TO	MOO-CHO
More	**Less**
Más	Menos
MahS	MĔ-NOS
Big	**Small**
Grande	Pequeño
GRahN-DĔ	PĔ-KĔN-YO

Open	**Closed**
Abierto	Cerrado
ah-BEE-eR-TO	Se-Rah-DO
Cheap	**Expensive**
Barato	Caro
Bah-Rah-TO	Kah-RO
Clean	**Dirty**
Limpio	Sucio
LEEM-PEE-O	Soo-SEE-O
Good	**Bad**
Bueno	Malo
BWe-NO	Mah-LO
Vacant	**Occupied**
Vacantes	Ocupado
Vah-Kah'N-Tes	O-Koo-Pah-DO
Right	**Wrong**
Correcto	Incorrecto
KO-ReK-TO	EEN-KO-ReK-TO

WORDS OF ENDEARMENT

I love you.

Te amo.

Tẽ ah-MO

My love

Mi amor

MEE ah-MOR

My life

Mi vida

MEE VEE-Dah

My friend (to a male)

Mi amigo

MEE ah-MEE-GO

My friend (to a female)

Mi amiga

MEE ah-MEE-Gah

Kiss me!

¡Bésame!

BE-Sah-ME

WORDS OF ANGER

What do you want?

¿Qué quiere usted?

Kē Kēē-ē´-Rē ⁰⁰S-Tē´D

Leave me alone!

¡Déjeme en paz!

Dē´-Hē-Mē ēN PₐₕS

Go away!

¡Váyase!

VῘ´-Yₐₕ-Sē

Stop bothering me!

¡No me moleste más!

N⁰ Mē M⁰-Lē´S-Tē MₐₕS

Be quiet!

¡Silencio!

Sēē-Lē´N-Sēē-⁰

That's enough!

¡Basta!

Bₐₕ´S-Tₐₕ

COMMON EXPRESSIONS

!!!

When you are at a loss for words but have the feeling you should say something, try one of these!

Who knows?

¿Quién sabe?

KEE-ẽN Sah-Bẽ

That's the truth!

¡Es verdad!

ẽS VẽR-Dah D

Sure!

¡Claro!

KLah-RO

Wow!

¡Caramba!

Kah-RahM-Bah

What's happening?

¿Qué pasa?

Kẽ Pah-Sah

I think so.

Creo que sí.

KRẽ-O Kẽ SEE

Cheers!

¡Salud!

SAH-LOOD

Good luck!

¡Buena suerte!

BWE-NAH SWER-TE

With pleasure!

¡Con mucho gusto!

KON MOO-CHO GOOS-TO

My goodness!

¡Dios mío!

DEE-OS MEE-O

What a shame! / That's too bad!

¡Qué lástima!

KE LAHS-TEE-MAH

Well done! Bravo!

¡Olé!

O-LA

Never mind!

¡Olvídelo!

OL-VEE-DE-LO

USEFUL COMMANDS

Stop!
¡Párese!

P**ah**-R**ĕ**-S**ĕ**

Go!
¡Vaya!

V**ah**-Y**ah**

Wait!
¡Espérese!

ĕS-P**ĕ**-R**ĕ**-S**ĕ**

Hurry!
¡Apúrese!

ah-P**oo**-R**ĕ**-S**ĕ**

Slow down!
¡Despacio!

D**ĕ**-SP**ah**-S** EE**-**O**

Come here!

¡Venga acá! (formal)   ¡Ven acá! (informal)

V**ĕ**N-G**ah**   **ah**-K**ah**   V**ĕ**N   **ah**-K**ah**

Help!
¡Socorro!

S**O**-K**O**-R**O**

EMERGENCIES

Fire!

¡Incendio!

ⒺⒺN-SⒺ́N-DⒺⒺ-Ⓞ

Emergency!

¡Emergencia!

Ⓔ́-MⒺⓇ-HⒺ́N-SⒺⒺ-ⓐⓗ

Call the police!

¡Llame a la policía!

Yⓐⓗ́-MⒺ ⓐⓗ Lⓐⓗ PⓄ-LⒺⒺ-SⒺⒺ́-ⓐⓗ

Call a doctor!

¡Llame un médico!

Yⓐⓗ́-MⒺ ⓄⓄN MⒺ́-DⒺⒺ-KⓄ

Call an ambulance!

¡Llame una ambulancia!

Yⓐⓗ́-MⒺ ⓄⓄ́-Nⓐⓗ
ⓐⓗM-BⓄⓄ-Lⓐⓗ́N-SⒺⒺ-ⓐⓗ

I need help!

¡Necesito ayuda!

NⒺ́-SⒺ́-SⒺⒺ́-TⓄ ⓐⓗ-YⓄⓄ́-Dⓐⓗ

ARRIVAL

Passing through customs should be easy since there are usually agents available who speak English. You may be asked how long you intend to stay and if you have anything to declare.

- Have your passport ready.

- Be sure all documents are up-to-date.

- While in a foreign country, it is wise to keep receipts for everything you buy.

- Be aware that many countries will charge a departure tax when you leave. Your travel agent should be able to find out if this affects you.

- If you have connecting flights, be sure to reconfirm them in advance.

- Make sure your luggage is clearly marked inside and out.

- Take valuables and medicines in carry-on bags.

SIGNS TO LOOK FOR:

ADUANA (Customs)

FRONTERA (Border)

CONTROL DE EQUIPAJE (Baggage control)

KEY WORDS

Baggage

El equipaje

ⒺL Ⓔ-KⒺ-Pⓐ-Hⓔ

Customs

La aduana

Lⓐ ⓐ-DWⓐ-Nⓐ

Documents

Los documentos

LⓄS DⓄ-KⓄ-MⒺN-TⓄS

Passport

El pasaporte

ⒺL Pⓐ-Sⓐ-PⓄB-Tⓔ

Porter

El maletero   El mozo (Spain)

ⒺL Mⓐ-Lⓔ-Tⓔ-BⓄ   ⒺL MⓄ-THⓄ

In Spain the letter **z** is prounounced like the **th** in **th**ink.

Tax

Los impuestos

LⓄS ⒺM-PWⓔS-TⓄS

USEFUL PHRASES

Here is my passport.

Aquí tiene mi pasaporte.

ⓐⓗ-Ⓚ(EE)´ Ⓣ(EE)-(ĕ)´-Ⓝ(ĕ) Ⓜ(EE)
Ⓟⓐⓗ-Ⓢⓐⓗ-Ⓟ(O)´Ⓑ-Ⓣ(ĕ)

I have nothing to declare.

No tengo nada que declarar.

Ⓝ(O) Ⓣ(ĕ)´Ⓝ-Ⓖ(O) Ⓝⓐⓗ´-Ⓓⓐⓗ
Ⓚ(ĕ) Ⓓ(ĕ)-ⓀⓁⓐⓗ-Ⓡⓐⓗ´Ⓡ

I'm here on business.

Vengo de negocios.

Ⓥ(ĕ)´Ⓝ-Ⓖ(O) Ⓓ(ĕ) Ⓝ(ĕ)-Ⓖ(O)´-Ⓢ(EE)-(O)Ⓢ

I'm here on vacation.

Vengo de vacaciones.

Ⓥ(ĕ)´Ⓝ-Ⓖ(O) Ⓓ(ĕ) Ⓥⓐⓗ-Ⓚⓐⓗ-Ⓢ(EE)-(O)´-Ⓝ(ĕ)Ⓢ

Is there a problem?

¿Hay algún problema?

Ⓘ ⓐⓗⓁ-Ⓖ(oo)´Ⓝ ⓅⓇ(O)-ⒷⓁ(ĕ)´-Ⓜⓐⓗ

PHRASEMAKER

I'll be staying...

Me voy a quedar...

Mē Voy ah Kē-DahR...

▸ **one week**

una semana

oó-Nah Sē-Mah-Nah

▸ **two weeks**

dos semanas

DOS Sē-Mah-NahS

▸ **one month**

un mes

ooN Mē S

▸ **two months**

dos meses

DOS Mē S-ēS

USEFUL PHRASES

I need a porter!

¡Necesito un maletero!

N(ē)-S(ē)-S(EE)-T(O) (OO)N
M(ah)-L(ē)-T(ē)-R(O)

These are my bags.

Estas son mis maletas.

(ē)S-T(ah)S   S(O)N   M(EE)S   M(ah)-L(ē)-T(ah)S

I'm missing a bag.

Me falta una maleta.

M(ē)   F(ah)L-T(ah)   (OO)-N(ah)   M(ah)-L(ē)-T(ah)

Take my bags to the taxi, please.

Lleve mis maletas al taxi, por favor.

Y(ē)-V(ē)   M(EE)S   M(ah)-L(ē)-T(ah)S   (ah)L
T(ah)K-S(EE)   P(O)R   F(ah)-V(O)R

Thank you. This is for you.

Gracias. Esto es para usted.

GR(ah)-S(EE)-(ah)S
(ē)S-T(O)   (ē)S   P(ah)-R(ah)   (OO)S-T(ē)D

PHRASEMAKER

Where is…

¿Dónde está...

DⓄN-DⒺ ⒺS-TⓐⒽ...

▸ **customs?**

la aduana?

LⓐⒽ ⓐⒽ-DWⓐⒽ-NⓐⒽ

▸ **baggage claim?**

la reclamación de equipaje?

LⓐⒽ RⒺ-KLⓐⒽ-MⓐⒽ-SⒺⒺ-ⓄN
DⒺ Ⓔ-KⒺⒺ-PⓐⒽ-HⒺ

▸ **the money exchange?**

la casa de cambio?

LⓐⒽ KⓐⒽ-SⓐⒽ DⒺ KⓐⒽM-BⒺⒺ-Ⓞ

▸ **the taxi stand?**

la parada de taxis?

LⓐⒽ PⓐⒽ-RⓐⒽ-DⓐⒽ DⒺ TⓐⒽK-SⒺⒺS

▸ **the bus stop?**

la parada de autobuses?

LⓐⒽ-PⓐⒽ-RⓐⒽ-DⓐⒽ DⒺ
ⓄW-TⓄ-BⓄⓄ-SⒺS

HOTEL
SURVIVAL

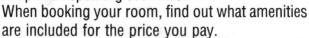

A wide selection of
accommodations, ranging
from the most basic to the
most extravagant, are
available wherever you travel
in Spanish-speaking countries.
When booking your room, find out what amenities
are included for the price you pay.

- Make reservations well in advance and get
  written confirmation of your reservations
  before you leave home.

- Always have identification ready when
  checking in.

- Do not leave valuables, prescriptions, or cash
  in your room when you are not there!

- Electrical items like blow-dryers may need an
  adapter. Your hotel may be able to provide
  one, but to be safe, take one with you.

- Although a service charge is usually included
  on your bill, it is customary to tip maids,
  bellhops, and doormen.

KEY WORDS

Hotel

El hotel

ẽL Ⓞ-Tẽ́L

Bellman

El botones

ẽL BⓄ-TⓄ́-Nẽ́S

Maid

La camarera

Lⓐ Kⓐ-Mⓐ-Rẽ́-Rⓐ

Message

El recado

ẽL Rẽ́-Kⓐ́-DⓄ

Reservation

La reservación

Lⓐ Rẽ́-SẽR-Vⓐ-SEE-Ⓞ́N

Room service

El servicio de habitación

ẽL SẽR-VEE-SEE-Ⓞ Dẽ́

ⓐ-BEE-Tⓐ-SEE-Ⓞ́N

CHECKING IN

My name is…

Me llamo…

Mē Yah-MO…

I have a reservation.

Tengo una reservación.

TēN-GO oo-Nah
Bē-SēR-Vah-SEE-ON

If you don't have a reservation, just say no before this phrase.

Have you any vacancies?

¿Tiene alguna habitación libre?

TEE-ē-Nē ahL-Goo-Nah
ah-BEE-Tah-SEE-ON LEE-BRē

What is the charge per night?

¿Cuánto es por noche?

KWahN-TO ēS POR NO-CHē

Is there room service?

¿Hay servicio de habitación?

I SēR-VEE-SEE-O Dē
ah-BEE-Tah-SEE-ON

PHRASEMAKER

I would like a room...

Quiero un cuarto… por favor

KEE-é-RO ooN KWah́R-TO… PFV

▶ **with a bath**

con un baño

KON ooN Bah́N-YO

▶ **with one bed**

con una cama

KON oó-Nah Kah́-Mah

▶ **with two beds**

con dos camas

KON DOS Kah́-Mah S

▶ **with a shower**

con una ducha

KON oó-Nah Doó-CHah

▶ **with a view**

con una vista

KON oó-Nah VEÉS-Tah

USEFUL PHRASES

Where is the dining room?

¿Dónde está el comedor?

DON-De eS-Tah eL
KO-Me-DOB

Are meals included?

¿Están las comidas incluidas?

eS-TahN LahS KO-MEE-DahS
EEN-KLOO-EE-DahS

What time is breakfast?

¿A qué hora es el desayuno?

ah Ke O-Bah eS eL
De-Sah-YOO-NO

What time is lunch?

¿A qué hora es la comida?

ah Ke O-Bah eS Lah
KO-MEE-Dah

What time is dinner?

¿A qué hora es la cena?

ah Ke O-Bah eS
Lah Se-Nah

My room key, please.

Mi llave de mi cuarto, por favor.

MEE YAH-VE DE MEE
KWAHR-TO PFV

Are there any messages for me?

¿Tengo algún recado?

TEN-GO AHL-GOON RE-KAH-DO

Please wake me at…

Me despierta a las…por favor

ME DES-PEE-ER-TAH
AH LAHS… PFV

6:00	6:30
seis	seis y media
SAS	SAS EE ME-DEE-ah

7:00	7:30
siete	siete y media
SEE-E-TE	SEE-E-TE EE ME-DEE-ah

8:00	8:30
ocho	ocho y media
O-CHO	O-CHO EE ME-DEE-ah

9:00	9:30
nueve	nueve y media
NWE-VE	NWE-VE EE ME-DEE-ah

PHRASEMAKER

I need…

Necesito…

Nẽ-Sẽ-SĒ-TO…

▸ **a babysitter**

una niñera

OO-Nah NEEN-Yẽ-Rah

▸ **a bellman**

un botones

OON BO-TO-Nẽs

▸ **more blankets**

más cobijas (mantas)

Mahs KO-BĒ-Hahs (Mahn-Tahs)

▸ **a hotel safe**

una caja fuerte

OO-Nah Kah-Hah FWẽR-Tẽ

▸ **ice cubes**

cubitos de hielo

KOO-BĒ-TOS Dẽ Yẽ-LO

▶ **an extra key**

otra llave

Ō-TRah Yah-Vē

▶ **a maid**

una camarera

ōō-Nah Kah-Mah-Rē-Rah

▶ **the manager**

el gerente

ēL Hē-Rēn-Tē

▶ **clean sheets**

sábanas limpias

Sah-Bah-Nahs LēēM-Pēē-ahs

▶ **soap**

jabón

Hah-Bōn

▶ **toilet paper**

papel higiénico

Pah-Pēl ēē-Hēē-ē-Nēē-Kō

▶ **more towels**

más toallas

Mahs Tō-ah-Yahs

PHRASEMAKER
(PROBLEMS)

There is no…

No hay…

N◎ ①…

▶ **electricity**

electricidad

◉-L◉K-TR◉-S◉-D◉D

▶ **heat**

calefacción

K◉-L◉-F◉K-S◉-O'N

▶ **hot water**

agua caliente

◉-GW◉　K◉-L◉-◉N-T◉

▶ **light**

luz

L◉S

▶ **toilet paper**

papel higiénico

P◉-P◉L　◉-H◉-◉-N◉-K◎

PHRASEMAKER
(SPECIAL NEEDS)

Do you have…

¿Tiene…

T☺-☺-N☺…

▶ **an elevator?**

un ascensor?

☺N ☺-S☺N-S☺B

▶ **a ramp?**

una rampa?

☺-N☺ B☺M-P☺

▶ **a wheel chair?**

una silla de ruedas?

☺-N☺ S☺-Y☺ D☺ B☺-☺-D☺S

▶ **facilities for the disabled?**

facilidades para los inválidos?

F☺-S☺-L☺-D☺-D☺S P☺-B☺ L☺S
☺N-V☺-L☺-D☺S

CHECKING OUT

The bill, please.

La cuenta, por favor.

Lah KWēN-Tah PFV

Is this bill correct?

¿Está bien la cuenta?

ēS-Tah BēE-ēN Lah KWēN-Tah

Do you accept credit cards?

¿Se aceptan tarjetas de crédito?

Sē ah-SēP-Tah N Tah B-Hē-Tah S
Dē KBē-Dē-TO

Could you have my luggage brought down?

¿Pueden bajarme el equipaje?

PWē-DēN Bah-Hah B-Mē ēL
ē-KEE-Pah-Hē

Can you call a taxi for me?

¿Puede llamarme un taxi?

PWĕ-Dĕ Yah-Mah́R-Mĕ
ooN Tah́K-SĒE

I had a very good time!

¡Me lo pasé muy bien!

Mĕ LOo Pah-Sĕ MWĒE BĒE-ĕN

Thanks for everything.

Gracias por todo.

GRah́-SĒE-ahS POoR TŌo-DOo

We'll see you next time.

Nos veremos la próxima.

NOoS Vĕ-Rĕ-MOoS Lah
PROoK-SĒE-Mah

Good-bye.

Adiós.

ah-DĒE-OoS

RESTAURANT SURVIVAL

The food available in Latin America and Spain is diverse. You will find a variety of tasty regional specialties. Mealtimes may be quite different than what you are used to!

- In Latin America and Spain, breakfast is usually served till 11 AM, lunch between 1 and 4 PM, and dinner from 9 PM till midnight. These are general guidelines and vary from country to country.

- In Spain, the Tasca bar offers appetizers or (**tapas**), a delicious way to fill the gap of time between lunch and dinner and a great way to meet people.

- A tip or service charge is often automatically included in your bill. Look for the words **Servicio Incluido**.

- In Mexico, avoid drinking tap water. Bottled water is available and recommended. In major hotels and restaurants, purified water is used; however, it is advisable to ask if your drink and or ice has been prepared with tap water.

KEY WORDS

Breakfast

El desayuno

ĕL DĕS-ah-Yoo-NO

Lunch

El almuerzo

ĕL ahL-MWĕR-SO

Dinner

La cena

Lah Sĕ-Nah

Waiter

El camarero

ĕL Kah-Mah-Rĕ-RO

Waitress

La camarera

Lah Kah-Mah-Rĕ-Rah

Restaurant

El restaurante

ĕL RĕS-Tow-RahN-Tĕ

USEFUL PHRASES

A table for…

Una mesa para…

ⓄⓄ-Nⓐⓗ   Mⓔ̆-Sⓐⓗ   Pⓐⓗ-Rⓐⓗ…

2	**4**	**6**
dos	cuatro	seis
DⓄS	KWⓐⓗ-TRⓄ	SⓐS

The menu, please.

La carta, por favor.

Lⓐⓗ   Kⓐⓗ-Rⓐⓗ   PFV

Separate checks, please.

Cuentas separadas, por favor.

KWⓔ̆N-TⓐⓗS   Sⓔ̆-Pⓐⓗ-Rⓐⓗ-DⓐⓗS   PFV

We are in a hurry.

Tenemos prisa.

Tⓔ̆-Nⓔ̆-MⓄS   PRⒺⒺ-Sⓐⓗ

What do you recommend?

¿Qué recomienda la casa?

Kⓔ̆   Rⓔ̆-KⓄ-MⒺⒺ-ⓔ̆N-Dⓐⓗ

Lⓐⓗ   Kⓐⓗ-Sⓐⓗ

Please bring me...

Tráigame... por favor

TRĪ-Gah-Mē... PFV

Please bring us...

Tráiganos... por favor

TRĪ-Gah-NOS... PFV

I'm hungry.

Tengo hambre.

TĒN-GO ahM-BRē

I'm thirsty.

Tengo sed.

TĒN-GO SēD

Is service included?

¿Está incluido el servicio?

ēS-Tah EEN-KLoo-EE-DO ēL
SēR-Vē-Sē-O

The bill, please.

La cuenta, por favor.

Lah KWēN-Tah PFV

In Spain, the menu prices are required by law to include the service charge. It is customary to leave an additional tip if you are happy with the service!

PHRASEMAKER

Ordering beverages is easy and a great way to practice your Spanish! In many foreign countries you will have to request ice with your drinks.

Please bring me...

Tráigame... por favor.

TRĪ'-G⒜-M⒠... PFV

▸ **coffee**	▸ **tea**
un café	un té
⒪N K⒜-F⒠'	⒪N T⒠

▸ **with cream**

con crema

K⒪N KR⒠-M⒜

▸ **with sugar**

con azúcar

K⒪N ⒜-S⒪'-K⒜R

▸ **with lemon**

con limón

K⒪N L⒠-M⒪'N

▸ **with ice**

con hielo

K⒪N Y⒠'-L⒪

Soft drinks

Los refrescos

LOS Rĕ-FRĔS-KOS

Milk

La leche

Lah LĔ-CHĕ

Hot chocolate

El chocolate caliente

ĔL CHO-KO-Lah-Tĕ Kah-LEE-ĕN-Tĕ

Juice

El jugo

ĔL HOO-GO

Orange juice

El jugo de naranja

ĔL HOO-GO Dĕ Nah-Rah́N-Hah

Ice water

El agua fría

ĔL ah́-GWah FRĔĔ-ah

Mineral water

El agua mineral

ĔL ah́-GWah MEE-Nĕ-Rah́L

AT THE BAR

Bartender

El cantinero

ⒺL KⓐN-TⒺ-NⒺ-ⓇO

The wine list, please.

La lista de vinos, por favor.

Lⓐ LⒺS-Tⓐ DⒺ VⒺ-NⓄS PFV

Cocktail

El cóctel

ⒺL KⓄK-TⒺL

On the rocks

Con hielo

KⓄN YⒺ-LⓄ

Straight

Sin hielo

SⒺN YⒺ-LⓄ

With lemon

Con limón

KⓄN LⒺ-MⓄN

PHRASEMAKER

I would like a glass of...

Quisiera un vaso de...

K(EE)-S(EE)-(ē)-R(ah) (oo)N V(ah)-S(O) D(ē)...

▸ **champagne**

champaña

CH(ah)M-P(ah)N-Y(ah)

▸ **beer**

cerveza

S(ē)R-V(ē)-S(ah)

▸ **wine**

vino

V(EE)-N(O) or B(EE)-N(O)

You will often hear the Spanish letter **v** pronounced like a soft English **b**.

▸ **red wine**

vino tinto

V(EE)-N(O) T(EE)N-T(O)

▸ **white wine**

vino blanco

V(EE)-N(O) BL(ah)N-K(O)

ORDERING BREAKFAST

In Latin America, breakfast can be extravagant. In Spain, breakfast is generally a simple meal consisting of coffee or tea and bread.

Bread

El pan

ⓔL Pⓐ𝐍

Toast

El pan tostado

ⓔL Pⓐ𝐍 Tⓞ-STⓐ-Dⓞ

---

with butter

con mantequilla

Kⓞ𝐍 Mⓐ𝐍-Tⓔ-KⒺⒺ-Yⓐ

---

with jam

con mermelada

Kⓞ𝐍 Mⓔℝ-Mⓔ-Lⓐ-Dⓐ

Cereal

El cereal

ⓔL Sⓔ-ℝⓔ-ⓐL

PHRASEMAKER

I would like…

Quisiera…

KEE-SEE-é-Rah…

▶ **two eggs…**

dos huevos…

DOS Wé-VOS…

▶ **scrambled**   ▶ **fried**

revueltos   fritos

Ré-VWéL-TOS   FREE-TOS

▶ **with bacon**

con tocino

KON TO-SEE-NO

▶ **with ham**

con jamón

KON Hah-MON

▶ **with potatoes**

con papas   con patatas (Spain)

KON Pah-Pahs   KON Pah-Tah-Tahs

LUNCH AND DINNER

Although you are encouraged to sample regional cuisines, it is important to be able to order foods you are familiar with. This section will provide phrases to help you.

I would like…

Quisiera…

K㉘-S㉘-㉘-R㉔…

We would like…

Quisiéramos…

K㉘-S㉘-㉘-R㉔-M㉔S

Bring us…

Nos trae... por favor.

N㉔S TR㉔-㉘… kk

The lady would like…

La señora quisiera…

L㉔ S㉘N-Y㉔-R㉔ K㉘-S㉘-㉘-R㉔…

The gentleman would like…

El señor quisiera…

㉘L S㉘N-Y㉔R K㉘-S㉘-㉘-R㉔…

STARTERS

Appetizers

Los entremeses

LOS ĕN-TRĕ-Mĕ´-SĕS

Bread and butter

El pan y la mantequilla

ĕL PahN EE Lah MahN-Tĕ-KEE´-Yah

Cheese

El queso

ĕL Kĕ´-SO

Fruit

La fruta

Lah FRoo´-Tah

Salad

La ensalada

Lah ĕN-Sah-Lah´-Dah

Soup

La sopa

Lah SO´-Pah

MEATS

Bacon

El tocino

ⓔL TⓄ-Sⓔⓔ-NⓄ

Beef

La carne de res

Lⓐ Kⓐ́R-Nⓔ Dⓔ Rⓔs

Beef steak

El bistec

ⓔL Bⓔⓔ-STⓔK

Ham

El jamón

ⓔL Hⓐ-MⓄ́N

Lamb

El cordero

ⓔL KⓄR-Dⓔ́-RⓄ

Pork

La carne de puerco   Las carnitas (Mexico)

Lⓐ Kⓐ́R-Nⓔ Dⓔ PWⓔ́R-KⓄ

Lⓐs Kⓐ́R-Nⓔⓔ-Tⓐs

Veal

La carne de ternera

Lⓐ Kⓐ́R-Nⓔ Dⓔ Tⓔ́R-Nⓔ́-Rⓐ

POULTRY

Baked chicken

El pollo al horno

ⓔL PⓄ-Yⓞ ⓐhL ⓄB-Nⓞ

Broiled chicken

El pollo a la parrilla

ⓔL PⓄ-Yⓞ ⓐh Lⓐh Pⓐh-BⒺⒺ-Yⓐh

Fried chicken

El pollo frito

ⓔL PⓄ-Yⓞ FBⒺⒺ-Tⓞ

Duck

El pato

ⓔL Pⓐh-Tⓞ

Goose

El ganso

ⓔL GⓐhN-Sⓞ

Turkey

El pavo   El guajolote (Mexico)

ⓔL Pⓐh-Vⓞ   ⓔL GWⓐh-HⓄ-LⓄ-Tⓔ

SEAFOOD

Fish
El pescado
ⓔL PⓔS-Kⓐ-DⓄ

Lobster
La langosta
Lⓐ LⓐN-GⓄ-STⓐ

Oysters
Las ostras
LⓐS ⓄS-TRⓐS

Salmon
El salmón
ⓔL SⓐL-MⓄN

Shrimp
Los camarones
LⓄS Kⓐ-Mⓐ-RⓄ-NⓔS

Trout
La trucha
Lⓐ TRⓄⓄ-CHⓐ

Tuna
El atún
ⓔL ⓐ-TⓄⓄN

OTHER ENTREES

Sandwich

La torta (Latin America)   El bocadillo (Spain)

L@h TOB-T@h   @L BO-K@h-D@E-YO

Hot dog

El hot dog

@L H@hT D@hG

Hamburger

La hamburguesa

L@h @hM-BooB-G@E-S@h

French fries

Las papas fritas or Las patatas fritas (Spain)

L@hS P@h-P@hS FB@E-T@hS

L@hS P@h-T@h-T@hS FB@E-T@hS

Pasta

La pasta

L@h P@hS-T@h

Pizza

La pizza

L@h P@E T-S@h

VEGETABLES

Carrots

Las zanahorias

L@S S@-N@-O'-REE-@S

Corn

El maíz

@L M@-EE'S

Mushrooms

Los hongos   Los champiñones (Spain)

L©S ©N-G©S L©S CH@M-P@N-YO'-N@S

Onions

Las cebollas

L@S S@-BO'-Y@S

Potato

La papa   La patata (Spain)

L@ P@'-P@   L@ P@-T@'-T@

Rice

El arroz

@L @-RO'S

Tomato

El tomate

@L TO-M@'-T@

FRUITS

Apple

La manzana

L@h M@hN-S@h'-N@h

Banana

La banana

L@h B@h-N@h'-N@h

Grapes

Las uvas

L@hS oo'-V@hS

Lemon

El limón

@L LEE-MON'

Orange

La naranja

L@h N@h-R@hN'-H@h

Strawberry

La fresa

L@h FR@'-S@h

Watermelon

La sandía

L@h S@hN-DEE'-@h

DESSERT

Desserts
Los Postres

L⦿S P⦿S-TR̃ⓔS

Apple pie
El pastel de manzana

ⓔL Pⓐ-STⓔL Dⓔ Mⓐ-N-Sⓐ-Nⓐ

Cherry pie
El pastel de cereza

ⓔL Pⓐ-STⓔL Dⓔ Sⓔ-R̃ⓔ-Sⓐ

Pastries
Los pasteles

L⦿S Pⓐ-STⓔ-LⓔS

Candy
Los dulces

L⦿S D⚭L-SⓔS

Ice cream

La nieve   El helado (Spain)

Lⓐⓗ Nⓔⓔ-ⓔ́-Vⓔ   ⓔL ⓔ-Lⓐⓗ́-DⓄ

Ice-cream cone

El barquillo de helado

ⓔL BⓐⓗR-Kⓔⓔ-YⓄ Dⓔ ⓔ-Lⓐⓗ́-DⓄ

Chocolate

El chocolate

ⓔL CHⓄ-KⓄ-Lⓐⓗ́-Tⓔ

Strawberry

La fresa

Lⓐⓗ FRⓔ́-Sⓐⓗ

Vanilla

La vainilla

Lⓐⓗ Vⓘ-Nⓔⓔ́-Yⓐⓗ

CONDIMENTS

Butter
La mantequilla
L(ah) M(ah)N-T(e)-K(EE)-Y(ah)

Ketchup
El ketchup
(e)L K(e)-CH(oo)P

Mayonnaise
La mayonesa
L(ah) M(ah)-Y(O)-N(e)-S(ah)

Mustard
La mostaza
L(ah) M(O)S-T(ah)-S(ah)

Salt	**Pepper**
La sal	La pimienta
L(ah) S(ah)L	L(ah) P(EE)-M(EE)-(e)N-T(ah)

Sugar
El azúcar
(e)L (ah)-S(oo)-K(ah)R

Vinegar and oil
El vinagre y aceite
(e)L V(EE)-N(ah)-GR(e) (EE) (ah)-S(A)-T(e)

SETTINGS

A cup

Una taza

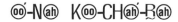OO-N@h T@h-S@h

A glass

Un vaso

@ON V@h-S@

A spoon

Una cuchara

OO-N@h K@-CH@h-R@h

A fork

Un tenedor

@ON T@-N@-D@R

A knife

Un cuchillo

@ON K@-CH@E-Y@

A plate

Un plato

@ON PL@h-T@

A napkin

Una servilleta

OO-N@h S@R-V@E-Y@-T@h

HOW DO YOU WANT IT COOKED?

Baked

Al horno

@L O'B-NO

Broiled

A la parrilla

@ L@ P@-B'EE-Y@

Steamed

Al vapor

@L V@-PO'B

Fried

Frito

FBEE-TO

Rare

Poco cocida

PO'-KO KO-SEE-D@

Medium

Término medio

TE'B-MEE-NO ME'-DEE-O

Well done

Bien cocida

BEE-E'N KO-SEE-D@

PROBLEMS

I didn't order this.

No pedí esto.

NO Pĕ-DEE ĕS-TO

Is the bill correct?

¿Está bien la cuenta?

ĕS-Tah BEE-ĕN Lah KWĕN-Tah

Please bring me...

Tráigame... por favor.

TRI-Gah-Mĕ... PFV

GETTING AROUND

Getting around in a foreign country can be an adventure in itself! Taxi and bus drivers do not always speak English, so it is essential to be able to give simple directions. The words and phrases in this chapter will help you get where you're going.

- Negotiate the fare with your taxi driver in advance so there are no misunderstandings. Tell him where you want to go and find out exactly what he intends to charge.

- Never get in unmarked taxi cabs no matter where you are!

- Check with your travel agent about special rail passes which allow unlimited travel within a set period of time.

- If you are traveling by train in Europe, remember trains leave on time. Arrive early to allow time for ticket purchasing and checking in.

- There are several types of train transportation from **Talgos** (fast) to **Rápidos** (regular) and **Estrellas** (nighttime). **Regionales** travel regionally, **Cercanas** are local commuter trains, and **Largo** are long-distance trains.

KEY WORDS

Airport

El aeropuerto

ⓔL ⓐ-ⓔ-ⓇⓄ-PWⓔR-TⓄ

Bus Station / Stop

La estación de autobuses

La parada de autobuses

Lⓐ ⓔ-STⓐ-SⒺ-ⓄN Dⓔ ⓄW-TⓄ-Bⓞⓞ-SⓔS

Lⓐ Pⓐ-Rⓐ-Dⓐ Dⓔ ⓄW-TⓄ-Bⓞⓞ-SⓔS

Car Rental Agency

Una agencia de carros de alquiler

ⓄⓄN-ⓐ ⓐ-Hⓔ'N-SⒺ-ⓐ Dⓔ

Kⓐ-RⓄS Dⓔ ⓐ-KⒺ-Lⓔ'R

Subway Station

La estación de metro

Lⓐ ⓔ-STⓐ-SⒺ-ⓄN Dⓔ Mⓔ-TRⓄ

Taxi Stand

La parada de taxis

Lⓐ Pⓐ-Rⓐ-Dⓐ Dⓔ Tⓐ'K-SⒺ

Train Station

La estación de ferrocarriles

Lⓐ ⓔ-STⓐ-SⒺ-ⓄN Dⓔ

Fⓔ-RⓄ-Kⓐ-Rⓔ'L-ⓔS

AIR TRAVEL

Arrivals
Las llegadas

L@S Y@-G@-D@S

Departures
Las salidas

L@S S@-L@-D@S

Flight number
El número de vuelo

@L N@-M@-R@ D@ VW@-L@

Airline
La línea aérea

L@ L@-N@-@ @-@-R@-@

The gate
La puerta

L@ PW@R-T@

Information
Información

@N-F@R-M@-S@-@N

Ticket (airline)
El boleto

@L B@-L@-T@

Reservations
Las reservaciones

L@S R@-S@R-V@-S@-@-N@S

PHRASEMAKER

I would like a seat...

Quisiera un asiento...

K(EE)-S(EE)-(ē)-R(ah) (OO)N (ah)-S(EE)-(ē)N-T(O)...

▶ **in first class**

en la sección de primera clase

(ē)N L(ah) S(ē)K-S(EE)-(O)N D(ē)
PR(EE)-M(ē)-R(ah) KL(ah)-S(ē)

▶ **next to the window**

cerca de la ventanilla

S(ē)R-K(ah) D(ē) L(ah) V(ē)N-T(ah)-N(EE)-Y(ah)

▶ **on the aisle**

en el pasillo

(ē)N (ē)L P(ah)-S(EE)-Y(O)

▶ **near the exit**

cerca de la salida

S(ē)R-K(ah) D(ē) L(ah) S(ah)-L(EE)-D(ah)

BY BUS

Bus

El autobús   El camión (Mexico)

ⓔL ⓞⓦ-TⓄ-BⓞⓞŚ   ⓔL Kⓐⓗ-Mⓔⓔ-ⓄN

Where is the bus stop?

¿Dónde está la parada de autobuses?

DⓄ́N-Dⓔ ⓔS-Tⓐⓗ́ Lⓐⓗ

Pⓐⓗ-Rⓐⓗ́-Dⓐⓗ Dⓔ ⓞⓦ-TⓄ-Bⓞⓞ́-Sⓔs

Do you go to…?

¿Va usted a…?

Vⓐⓗ ⓞⓞ-STⓔ́D ⓐⓗ…

What is the fare?

¿Cuál es la tarifa?

KWⓐⓗL ⓔS Lⓐⓗ Tⓐⓗ-Rⓔⓔ́-Fⓐⓗ

Do I need exact change?

¿Necesito tener cambio exacto?

Nⓔ-Sⓔ́-Sⓔⓔ́-TⓄ Tⓔ-Nⓔ́R

Kⓐⓗ́M-Bⓔⓔ-Ⓞ ⓔK-Sⓐⓗ́K-TⓄ

How often do the buses run?

¿Cada cuándo pasan los autobuses?

Kⓐⓗ́-Dⓐⓗ KWⓐⓗ́N-DⓄ Pⓐⓗ-Sⓐⓗ́N

LⓄS ⓞⓦ-TⓄ-Bⓞⓞ́-SⓔS

PHRASEMAKER

Please tell me...

Dígame... por favor.

DEE-Gah-Mē... PFV

▸ **which bus goes to...**

cuál autobús va para...

KWah L ow-TO-Boo'S Vah Pah-Rah...

▸ **at what time does the bus leave**

a qué hora sale el autobús

ah Kē O'-Rah Sah'-Lē
ēL ow-TO-Boo'S

▸ **where the bus stop is**

dónde está la parada de autobuses

DON-Dē ēS-Tah' Lah Pah-Rah'-Dah
Dē ow-TO-Boo'-SēS

▸ **when we are at...**

cuando estemos en...

KWah N-DO ēS-Tē-MOS ēN...

▸ **where to get off**

dónde debo bajarme

DON-Dē Dē'-BO Bah-Hah'R-Mē

BY CAR

Fill it up.

Llénelo.

YḖ-NĒ-LO

Can you help me?

¿Puede usted ayudarme?

PWḖ-DĒ ⓞⓞS-TḖD
ⓐⓗ-Yⓞⓞ-DⓐⓗʹR-MĒ

My car won't start.

Mi carro no arranca.

MEE Kⓐⓗʹ-RO NO ⓐⓗ-RⓐⓗN-Kⓐⓗ

Can you fix it?

¿Pueden arreglarlo?

PWḖ-DĒN ⓐⓗ-RĒ-GLⓐⓗʹR-LO

What will it cost?

¿Cuánto costará?

KWⓐⓗʹN-TO KO-STⓐⓗ-Rⓐⓗʹ

How long will it take?

¿Cuánto tiempo durará?

KWⓐⓗN-TO TEE-ḖM-PO Dⓞⓞ-Rⓐⓗ-Rⓐⓗʹ

PHRASEMAKER

Please check…

Revise… por favor.

R͟ē-Vēē-Sē… PFV

▸ **the battery**

la batería

Lah Bah-Tē-Rēē-ah

▸ **the brakes**

los frenos

L⊙S FRē-N⊙S

▸ **the oil**

el aceite

ēL ah-Sā-Tē

▸ **the tires**

las llantas

Lah S YahʹN-Tah S

▸ **the water**

el agua

ēL ahʹ-GWah

SUBWAYS AND TRAINS

Where is the subway station?

¿Dónde está el metro?

DŌN-Dē ēS-Tah ēL Mē-TRO

Where is the train station?

¿Dónde está la estación de ferrocarril?

DŌN-Dē ēS-Tah Lah

ēS-Tah-SEE-ŌN Dē Fē-RO-Kah-RēL

A one-way ticket, please.

Un billete de ida, por favor.

ooN BEE-Yē-Tē Dē EE-Dah PFV

A round trip ticket

Un billete de ida y vuelta

ooN BEE-Yē-Tē Dē EE-Dah

EE VWēL-Tah PFV

First class

Primera clase

PREE-Mē-Rah KLah-Sē

Second class

Segunda clase

Sē-GooN-Dah KLah-Sē

Which train do I take to go to…

¿Cuál tren tomo para ir a…?

KWaL TReN TO-MO
Pah-Rah EER ah…

What is the fare?

¿Cuánto es la tarifa?

KWaN-TO eS Lah Tah-REE-Fah

Is this seat taken?

¿Está ocupado este asiento?

eS-Tah O-Koo-Pah-DO
eS-Te ah-SEE-eN-TO

Do I have to change trains?

¿Tengo que cambiar de tren?

TeN-GO Ke KahM-BEE-ahR
De TReN

Does this train stop at…?

¿Se para este tren en…?

Se Pah-Rah eS-Te TReN eN…

Where are we?

¿Dónde estamos?

DON-De eS-Tah-MOS

BY TAXI

Can you call a taxi for me?

¿Me puede llamar un taxi?

M⑥ PW⑥-D⑥ Y⑩-M⑩R
⑩N T⑩K-S⑥

Are you available?

¿Está usted libre?

⑥S-T⑩ ⑩S-T⑥D L⑥-BR⑥

I want to go…

Quiero ir…

K⑥-⑥-R⑥ ⑥R…

Stop here, please.

Pare aquí, por favor.

P⑩-R⑥ ⑩-K⑥ PFV

Please wait.

Espérese, por favor.

⑥-SP⑥-R⑥-S⑥ PFV

How much do I owe?

¿Cuánto le debo?

KW⑩N-T⑩ L⑥ D⑥-B⑥

PHRASEMAKER

I would like to go…

Quisiera ir…

K₢-S₢-ē´-R₳ ₢R…

▸ **to this address**

a esta dirección

₳ ē´S-T₳ D₢-R₢K-S₢-O´N

▸ **to the airport**

al aeropuerto

₳L ₳-ē-R◯-PW₢R-T◯

▸ **to the bank**

al banco

₳L B₳N-K◯

▸ **to the hotel**

al hotel

₳L ◯-Tē´L

▸ **to the hospital**

al hospital

₳L ◯S-P₢-T₳´L

▸ **to the subway station**

al metro

₳L Mē´-TR◯

SHOPPING

Whether you plan a major shopping
spree or just need to purchase
some basic necessities, the
following information is useful.

- In Latin America and Spain,
  shops generally close in the
  afternoon for siesta. They re-
  open in the late afternoon and stay open
  into the night.

- You are likely to encounter an item called VAT
  (in Mexico IVA). This stands for Value-Added
  Tax. It is a tax which is quoted in the price
  of merchandise and services. Unlike other
  countries, Mexico's IVA is not refundable.

- In Spain, always inquire about VAT refund
  procedures at the time of purchase.

- Always keep receipts for everything you buy!
  This will be helpful in filling out Customs
  declaration forms when you return home.

SIGNS TO LOOK FOR:

ALMACEN (Department Store)

BAZAR (Department Store, Spain)

PANADERIA (Bakery)

MERCADO (Market)

SUPERMERCADO (Supermarket)

KEY WORDS

Credit card

La tarjeta de crédito

L@ T@R-H@-T@ D@ KR@-D@-T@

Money

El dinero

@L D@-N@-R@

Receipt

El recibo

@L R@-S@-B@

Sale

La venta

L@ V@N-T@

Store

La tienda

L@ T@-@N-D@

Traveler's check

El cheque de viajero

@L CH@-K@ D@ V@-@-H@-R@

USEFUL PHRASES

Do you sell…?

¿Vende usted…?

V@N-D@ @S-T@D…

Do you have…?

¿Tiene usted…?

T@-@-N@ @S-T@D…

I want to buy…

Quisiera comprar…

K@-S@-@-R@ K@M-PR@R…

How much?

¿Cuánto es?

KW@N-T@ @S

When are the shops open?

¿Cuándo se abren las tiendas?

KW@N-D@ S@ @-BR@N
L@S T@-@N-D@S

No thank you.

No, gracias.

N@ GR@-S@-@S

I´m just looking.

Sólo estoy mirando.

SO-LO ES-TOY MEE-Bah-N-DO

It's very expensive!

¡Es muy caro!

ES MWEE Kah-BO

Can't you give me a discount?

¿No me da una rebaja?

NO ME Dah oo-Nah Be-Bah-Hah

I'll take it!

¡Me lo llevo!

ME LO YE-VO

I'd like a receipt, please.

Quiero un recibo, por favor.

KEE-e-BO oN Be-SEE-BO PFV

I want to return this.

Quiero devolver esto.

KEE-e-BO De-VOL-VeB eS-TO

It doesn't fit.

No me viene.

NO ME VEE-e-Ne

PHRASEMAKER

I'm looking for…

Busco…

B⓪S-K⓪…

▶ **a bakery**

una panadería

⓪-Nⓐ Pⓐ-Nⓐ-D⑥-R⑥-ⓐ

▶ **a bank**

un banco

⓪N BⓐN-K⓪

▶ **a barber shop**

una peluquería

⓪-Nⓐ P⑥-L⓪-K⑥-R⑥-ⓐ

▶ **a beauty shop**

un salón de belleza

⓪N Sⓐ-L⓪N D⑥ B⑥-Y⑥-Sⓐ

▶ **a camera shop**

una tienda de fotografía

⓪N-ⓐ T⑥-⑥N-Dⓐ D⑥

F⓪-T⓪-GRⓐ-F⑥-ⓐ

▶ **a pharmacy**

una farmacia

⓪-Nⓐ FⓐR-Mⓐ-S⑥-ⓐ

PHRASEMAKER

Do you sell...

Vende usted…

V@́N-D@ @S-T@́D...

▶ **aspirin?**

aspirinas?

@-SP@-R@́-N@S

▶ **cigarettes?**

cigarrillos?

S@-G@-R@́-Y@S

▶ **deodorant?**

desodorante?

D@-S@-D@-R@N-T@

▶ **dresses?**

vestidos?

V@-ST@́-D@S

▶ **film?**

rollo de cámara?

R@́-Y@ D@ K@-M@-R@

▶ **pantyhose?**

pantimedias?

P@N-T©©-M©́-D©©-@S

▶ **perfume?**

perfume?

P©R-F©o-M©

▶ **razor blades?**

hojas de afeitar?

Ó-H@S D© @-F©́-T@R

▶ **shampoo?**

champú?

CH@M-P©o

▶ **shaving cream?**

crema de afeitar?

KR©́-M@ D© @-F©́-T@R

▶ **shirts?**

camisas?

K@-M©©́-S@S

▶ **soap?**

jabón?

H@-BÓN

▸ **sunglasses?**

anteojos para el sol?

ahN-Tĕ-O-HOS Pah-Rah ĕL SOL

▸ **sunscreen?**

aceite para broncear?

ah-SA-Tĕ Pah-Rah

BRON-Sĕ-ahR

▸ **toothbrushes?**

cepillos de dientes?

Sĕ-PEE-YOS Dĕ DEE-ĕN-TĕS

▸ **toothpaste?**

pasta de dientes?

PahS-Tah Dĕ DEE-ĕN-TĕS

▸ **water?** (bottled)

agua de botella?

ah-GWah Dĕ BO-Tĕ-Yah

▸ **water?** (mineral)

agua mineral?

ah-GWah MEE-Nĕ-RahL

ESSENTIAL SERVICES

THE BANK

As a traveler in a foreign country your primary contact with banks will be to exchange money.

- Change enough funds before leaving home to pay for tips, food, and transportation to your final destination.

- It is also best to bring US dollar or Euro traveler's checks as well as some currency in cash. You can exchange money in banks or **Casas de Cambio.**

- Current exchange rates are posted in banks and published daily in city newspapers.

- ATM machines are readily available in Mexico and are always open. Try to use ATMs in daylight hours. Credit cards are accepted widely.

- ATM machines are readily available in Spain and a good place to obtain Euros. Credit cards are accepted and purchases usually provide a favorable rate of exchange.

KEY WORDS

Bank

El banco

ⓔL Bⓐ️N-Kⓞ

Exchange office

La casa de cambio

Lⓐ Kⓐ-Sⓐ Dⓔ Kⓐ️M-BⒺⒺ-ⓞ

Money

El dinero

ⓔL DⒺⒺ-Nⓔ-Rⓞ

Money order

El giro postal

ⓔL HⒺⒺ-Rⓞ PⓞS-Tⓐ️L

Travelers checks

Cheque de viajero

CHⓔ-KⓔS Dⓔ VⒺⒺ-ⓐ-Hⓔ-Rⓞ

Currencies

Peso/Mexico	Euro/Spain	Sol/Perú
Pⓔ-Sⓞ	ⓞⓞ-Rⓞ	SⓞL
Balboa/Panamá	Colón/El Salvador	Peso/Chile
Bⓐ️L-Bⓞ-ⓐ	Kⓞ-Lⓞ́N	Pⓔ-Sⓞ

USEFUL PHRASES

Where is the bank?

¿Dónde está el banco?

DON-D(e) (e)S-T(ah) (e)L B(ah)N-K(o)

What time does the bank open?

¿A qué hora abre el banco?

(ah) K(e) (o)-R(ah) (ah)-BR(e)
(e)L B(ah)N-K(o)

Where is the exchange office?

¿Dónde está la casa de cambio?

DON-D(e) (e)S-T(ah) L(ah) K(ah)-S(ah)
D(e) K(ah)M-B(ee)-(o)

What time does the exchange office open?

¿A qué hora abre la casa de cambio?

(ah) K(e) (o)-R(ah) (ah)-BR(e) L(ah)
K(ah)-S(ah) D(e) K(ah)M-B(ee)-(o)

Can I change dollars here?

¿Puedo cambiar dólares aquí?

PW(e)-D(o) K(ah)M-B(ee)-(ah)R
D(o)-L(ah)-R(e)S (ah)-K(ee)

Can you change this?

¿Me puede cambiar esto?

Mⓔ PWⓔ́-Dⓔ Kⓐ̇M-BⓔⒺ-ⓐ̇R ⓔ́S-Tⓞ

What is the exchange rate?

¿A cuánto está el cambio?

ⓐ KWⓐ̇N-Tⓞ ⓔ́S-Tⓐ̇ ⓔL
Kⓐ̇M-BⓔⒺ-ⓞ

I would like large bills.

Quisiera billetes grandes.

KⒺⒺ-SⒺⒺ-ⓔ́-Rⓐ̇ BⒺⒺ-Yⓔ́-Tⓔ́S
GRⓐ̇́N-Dⓔ́S

I would like small bills.

Quisiera billetes pequeños.

KⒺⒺ-SⒺⒺ-ⓔ́-Rⓐ̇ BⒺⒺ-Yⓔ́-Tⓔ́S
Pⓔ́-Kⓔ́N-Yⓞ̇S

I need change.

Necesito cambio.

Nⓔ̇-Sⓔ̇-SⒺⒺ-Tⓞ Kⓐ̇M-BⓔⒺ-ⓞ

Do you have an ATM?

¿Tienen cajero automático?

TⒺⒺ́-ⓔ̇-Nⓔ̇N Kⓐ̇-Hⓔ̇R-ⓞ
ⓦ-Tⓞ-Mⓐ̇́-TⒺⒺ-Kⓞ

POST OFFICE

If you are planning to send letters and postcards, be sure to send them early so that you don't arrive home before they do. **Correo** identifies the post office.

KEY WORDS

Airmail

Por avión

POR ah-VEE-ON

Letter

La carta

Lah KAR-Tah

Post office

El correo

EL KO-REe-O

Postcard

La tarjeta postal

Lah TaR-Hee-Tah POS-TaL

Stamp

El sello

EL SEe-YO

USEFUL PHRASES

Where is the post office?

¿Dónde está el correo?

DON-De eS-Tah eL KO-Re-O

What time does the post office open?

¿A qué hora abren los correos?

ah Ke O-Rah ahB-ReN
LOS KO-Re-OS

I need stamps.

Necesito unos sellos.

Ne-Se-See-TO oo-NOS Se-YOS

I need an envelope.

Necesito un sobre.

Ne-Se-See-TO ooN SO-BRe

I need a pen.

Necesito una pluma.

Ne-Se-See-TO oo-Nah PLoo-Mah

TELEPHONE

Placing phone calls in a foreign country can be a test of will and stamina! Besides the obvious language barriers, service can vary greatly from one town to the next.

- If you have a choice, do not call from your hotel room. Service charges can add a hefty amount to your bill. If you use your hotel for long distance or international calls, use a Calling Card. This will cost you less than hotel charges; however, a fee may still be charged.

- In Spain, try to get to the CENTRAL TELEFONICA (CTNE). Here you can get assistance placing your call. You pay as soon as the call is completed.

- Calls can be made at telephone call centers and paid afterwards. There are also telephones in bars which cost more to use.

- In Mexico, you can purchase calling cards in stores, supermarkets, and newsstands. They can be used in "yellow" Telmex/Ladatel phone booths.

KEY WORDS

Information

Información

ⒺN-FⓄR-Mⓐ-SⒺ-ⓄN

Long distance

Larga distancia

Lⓐ́R-Gⓐ   DⒺS-Tⓐ́N-SⒺ-ⓐ

Operator

La operadora

Lⓐ   Ⓞ-Pⓔ́-Rⓐ-DⓄ́R-ⓐ

Phone book

La guía telefónica

Lⓐ   GⒺ́-ⓐ   Tⓔ-Lⓔ́-FⓄ́-NⒺ-Kⓐ

Public telephone

Teléfono público

Tⓔ́-Lⓔ́-FⓄ-NⓄ   PⓄⓄB-LⒺ́-KⓄ

Telephone

El teléfono

ⓔL   Tⓔ́-Lⓔ́-FⓄ-NⓄ

USEFUL PHRASES

May I use your telephone?

¿Puedo usar su teléfono?

PWĕ-DO ⓞⓞ-Sⓐ'R Sⓞⓞ
Tⓔ-Lⓔ'-Fⓞ-Nⓞ

Operator, I don't speak Spanish.

Operadora, no hablo español.

ⓞ-Pⓔ-Rⓐ-DⓄ'R-ⓐ NⓄ ⓐ'B-LⓄ
ⓔS-Pⓐ'N-YⓄ'L

I would like to make a long-distance call.

Quisiera hacer una llamada de larga distancia.

Kⓔⓔ-Sⓔⓔ-ⓔ'-Rⓐ ⓐ-Sⓔ'R ⓞⓞ'-Nⓐ
Yⓐ-Mⓐ'-Dⓐ Dⓔ Lⓐ'R-Gⓐ
DⓔⓔS-Tⓐ'NSⓔⓔ-ⓐ

I would like to make a call to the United States.

Quisiera hacer una llamada a los Estados Unidos.

Kⓔⓔ-Sⓔⓔ-ⓔ'-Rⓐ ⓐ-Sⓔ'R ⓞⓞ'-Nⓐ
Yⓐ-Mⓐ'-Dⓐ ⓐ LⓄS ⓔS-Tⓐ'-DⓄS
ⓞⓞ-Nⓔⓔ'-DⓄS

I want to call this number...

Quiero llamar a este número...

KEE-é-RO Yah-MahR ah é-S-Té
NOO-MÉ-RO...

1	2	3
uno	dos	tres
OO-NO	DOS	TRéS
4	5	6
cuatro	cinco	seis
KWah-TRO	SEEN-KO	SAS
7	8	9
siete	ocho	nueve
SEE-é-Té	O-CHO	NWé-Vé
*	0	#
	cero	
	Sé-RO	

SIGHTSEEING AND ENTERTAINMENT

In most cities and towns in Spanish-speaking countries, you will find tourist information offices. Here you can usually obtain brochures, maps, historical information, bus and train schedules.

CITIES IN MEXICO

Ciudad de México
SEE-oo-DahD Deh Meh-HEE-KO

Acapulco
ah-Kah-POoL-KO

Cancún
KahN-KooN

CITIES IN SOUTH AMERICA

Buenos Aires
BWeh-NOS I-Reh's

Santiago
SahN-TEE-ah-GO

Bogotá
BO-GO-Tah'

Lima
LEE-Mah

CITIES IN SPAIN

Madrid
Mah-DREE'D

Barcelona
BahR-THeh-LO'-Nah

Sevilla (Seville)
Seh-VEE'-Yah

Pamplona
PahM-PLO'-Nah

KEY WORDS

Admission

La admisión

Lah ahD-MEE-SEE-OᐟN

Map

El mapa

ēL Mahᐟ-Pah

Reservation

La reservación

Lah Rē-SēR-Vah-SEE-OᐟN

Ticket

El boleto   El billete

ēL BO-Lēᐟ-TO   ēL BEE-Yēᐟ-Tē

Tour

La excursión

Lah ēKS-KooR-SEE-OᐟN

Tour guide

El guía turístico

ēL GEEᐟ-ah Too-REEᐟS-TEE-KO

USEFUL PHRASES

Where is the tourist office?

¿Dónde está la oficina de turismo?

DON-De eS-Tah Lah

O-Fee-SEE-Nah De Too-REEZ-MO

Is there a tour to…?

¿Hay una excursión a…?

I oo-Nah eKS-Koor-SEE-ON ah…

Where do I buy a ticket?

¿Dónde compro la entrada?

DON-De KOM-PRO Lah

eN-TRah-Dah

How much does the tour cost?

¿Cuánto cuesta la excursión?

KWahN-TO KWeS-Tah Lah

eKS-Koor-SEE-ON

How long does the tour take?

¿Cuánto dura la excursión?

KWahN-TO Doo-Rah Lah

eKS-Koor-SEE-ON

Does the guide speak English?

¿Habla inglés el guía?

ⓐⷢ-BLⓐ ⒺN-GLⓔⷢS ⒺL Gⓔⷢ-ⓐ

Are children free?

¿Pagan los niños?

Pⓐⷢ-GⓐⷢN LⓄS NⓔⷢN-YⓄS

What time does the show start?

¿A qué hora empieza la función?

ⓐ Kⓔ Ⓞⷢ-Rⓐ ⓔM-Pⓔⷢ-ⓔⷢ-Sⓐ
Lⓐ FⓄⓄN-Sⓔ-ⓄⷢN

Do I need reservation?

¿Necesito una reserva?

Nⓔⷢ-Sⓔⷢ-Sⓔⷢ-TⓄ ⓄⓄⷢ-Nⓐ
Rⓔⷢ-SⓔⷢR-Vⓐ

Where can we go dancing?

¿Dónde está la disco?

DⓄⷢN-Dⓔ ⓔⷢS-Tⓐⷢ Lⓐ DⓔⷢS-KⓄ

Is there a minimum cover charge?

¿Hay un cargo mínimo?

Ⓘ ⓄⓄN KⓐⷢR-GⓄ Mⓔⷢ-Nⓔⷢ-MⓄ

PHRASEMAKER

May I invite you…

¿Quisiera invitarla…

KEE-SEE-ê´-Rah EEN-VEE-TahR-Lah…

▶ **to a concert?**

a un concierto?

ah ooN KON-SEE-ê´R-TO

▶ **to dance?**

a bailar?

ah BI-L-ah´R

▶ **to dinner?**

a cenar?

ah Sê-Nah´R

▶ **to the movies?**

al cine?

ahL SEE´-Nê

▶ **to the theater?**

al teatro?

ahL Tê-ah´-TRO

PHRASEMAKER

Where can I find...

¿Dónde se encuentra...

DON-De Se eN-KWeN-TRah...

▶ **a health club?**

un gimnasio?

ooN HeeM-Nah-See-O

▶ **a swimming pool?**

una piscina?

oo-Nah PEE-SEE-Nah

▶ **a tennis court?**

una cancha de tenis?

oo-Nah Kah N-CHah De Te-NEES

▶ **a golf course?**

un campo de golf?

ooN Kah M-PO De GOLF

HEALTH

Hopefully you will not need medical attention on your trip. If you do, it is important to communicate basic information regarding your condition.

- Check with your insurance company before leaving home to find out if you are covered in a foreign country. You may want to purchase traveler's insurance before leaving home.

- If you take prescription medicine, carry your prescription with you. Have your prescriptions translated before you leave home.

- Take a small first-aid kit with you.

- Your embassy or consulate should be able to assist you in finding health care.

- In Mexico, some pharmacies are open 24 hours and others close around 10:00 PM.

- Some hotels can recommend English-speaking doctors and others have a doctor on call.

- In Spain, a **GREEN CROSS** indicates a pharmacy, where you can get basic medical information.

KEY WORDS

Ambulance

La ambulancia

L@h @hM-B@@-L@hN-S@E-@h

Dentist

El dentista

@L D@N-T@E'S-T@h

Doctor

El médico

@L M@'-D@E-K@

Emergency

La emergencia

L@h @-M@R-H@N-S@E-@h

Hospital

El hospital

@L @S-P@E-T@h'L

Prescription

La receta

L@h R@-S@'-T@h

USEFUL PHRASES

I am sick.

Estoy enfermo. (male)

ⒺS-Tⓞⓨ́ ⒺN-FⒺR-MⓄ

I am sick.

Estoy enferma. (female)

ⒺS-Tⓞⓨ́ ⒺN-FⒺR-Mⓐⓗ

I need a doctor.

Necesito un médico.

NⒺ-SⒺ-SⒺⒺ́-TⓄ ⓄⓄN MⒺ́-DⒺⒺ-KⓄ

It's an emergency!

¡Es una emergencia!

ⒺS ⓄⓄ́-Nⓐⓗ Ⓔ-MⒺR-HⒺN-SⒺⒺ-ⓐⓗ

Where is the nearest hospital?

¿Dónde está el hospital más cercano?

DⓄ́N-DⒺ ⒺS-Tⓐⓗ́ ⒺL ⓄS-PⒺⒺ-Tⓐⓗ́L
Mⓐⓗ́S SⒺR-Kⓐⓗ́-NⓄ

Call an ambulance!

¡Llame una ambulancia!

Yⓐⓗ́-MⒺ ⓄⓄ́-Nⓐⓗ ⓐⓗM-BⓄⓄ-Lⓐⓗ́N-SⒺⒺ-ⓐⓗ

I'm allergic to…

Tengo alergias a…

TĕN-GO ah-LĕR-HEE-ahS ah...

I'm pregnant.

Estoy embarazada.

ĕS-Toy ĕM-Bah-Rah-Sah-Dah

I'm diabetic.

Soy diabético. (male)

Soy DEE-ah-Bĕ-TEE-KO

I'm diabetic.

Soy diabética. (female)

Soy DEE-ah-Bĕ-TEE-Kah

I have a heart condition.

Sufro del corazón.

Soo-FRO DĕL KO-Rah-SON

I have high blood pressure.

Tengo la presión alta.

TĕN-GO Lah PRĕ-SEE-ON ahL-Tah

I have low blood pressure.

Tengo la presión baja.

TĕN-GO Lah PRĕ-SEE-ON Bah-Hah

PHRASEMAKER

I need…

Necesito…

Nẽ-Sẽ-SĒ-TO…

▸ **a doctor**

un médico

ⓄN Mẽ-DĒ-KO

▸ **a dentist**

un dentista

ⓄN DẽN-TĒS-Tah

▸ **a nurse**

una enfermera

Ⓞ-Nah ẽN-FẽR-Mẽ-Rah

▸ **an optician**

un optometrista

ⓄN ⓄP-TO-Mẽ-TRĒS-Tah

▸ **a pharmacist**

un farmacéutico

ⓄN FahR-Mah-SŌ-TĒ-KO

PHRASEMAKER
(AT THE PHARMACY)

Do you have…

¿Tiene usted…

TEE-ẽ´-Nẽ ⁰⁰S-TẽD…

▸ **aspirin?**

aspirinas?

@S-PEE-REE´-N@S

▸ **Band-Aids?**

curitas?

K⁰⁰-REE´-T@S

▸ **cough syrup?**

calmante de la tos?

K@L-M@N-Tẽ Dẽ L@ TOS

▸ **ear drops?**

gotas para los oídos?

GO´-T@S P@-R@ LOS O-EE-DOS

▸ **eyedrops?**

gotas para los ojos?

GO´-T@S P@-R@ LOS O´-HOS

BUSINESS TRAVEL

It is important to show appreciation and interest in another person's language and culture, particularly when doing business. A few well-pronounced phrases can make a great impression.

I have an appointment.

Tengo una cita.

TĔN-GŌ ŌŌ-Nah SĔE-Tah

Here is my card.

Aquí tiene mi tarjeta personal.

ah-KĒE TĒE-ĕ-NĔ MĒE
Tah-Hĕ-Tah PĔR-SO-Nah'L

Can we get an interpreter?

¿Hay un intérprete?

Ī ŌŌN ĒEN-TĔR-PRĔ-TĔ

May I speak to Mr…?

¿Se encuentra el señor…?

SĔ ĔN-KWĔN-TRah ĔL SĔN-YŌR…

May I speak to Mrs…?

¿Se encuentra la señora…?

SĔ ĔN-KWĔN-TRah Lah SĔN-YŌ-Rah…

KEY WORDS

Appointment

La cita

L@h S@E-T@h

Mr.

El señor

@L S@N-Y@B

Mrs.

La señora

L@h S@N-Y@-B@h

Meeting

La reunión

L@h B@-@N-Y@N

Marketing

El mercado técnico

@L M@B-K@h-D@ T@K-N@E-K@

Presentation

La presentación

L@h PB@-S@N-T@h-S@E-@N

Sales

Las ventas

L@hS V@N-T@hS

PHRASEMAKER

I need…

Necesito…

N⊕-S⊕-S⊕-T⊕…

▶ **a computer**

una computadora
un ordenador (Spain)

⊕-Nah K⊕M-P⊕-Tah-D⊕-Rah

⊕N ⊕R-D⊕-Nah-D⊕R

▶ **a copy machine**

una máquina para hacer copias

⊕-Nah Mah-K⊕-Nah Pah-Rah

ah-S⊕R K⊕-P⊕-ahS

▶ **a conference room**

un salón de conferencias

⊕N Sah-L⊕N D⊕ K⊕N-F⊕-R⊕N-S⊕-ahS

▶ **a fax machine**

un fax

⊕N Fah KS

▶ **an interpreter**

un intérprete

⊕N ⊕N-T⊕R-PR⊕-T⊕

▶ **a lawyer**

un abogado

ⓞⓞN ⓐⓗ-Bⓞ-Gⓐⓗ-Dⓞ

▶ **a notary**

un notario

ⓞⓞN Nⓞ-Tⓐⓗ-RⒺⒺ-ⓞ

▶ **overnight delivery**

entrega expresa
entrega inmediata (Spain)

ⓔN-TRⒺ-Gⓐⓗ ⒺKS-PRⒺ-Sⓐⓗ

ⓔN-TRⒺ-Gⓐⓗ ⒺⒺN-MⒺ-DⒺⒺ-ⓐⓗ-Tⓐⓗ

▶ **paper**

papel

Pⓐⓗ-PⒺL

▶ **pen** ▶ **pencil**

pluma lápiz

PLⓞⓞ-Mⓐⓗ Lⓐⓗ-PⒺⒺZ

▶ **a secretary**

una secretaria

ⓞⓞ-Nⓐⓗ SⒺ-KRⒺ-Tⓐⓗ-RⒺⒺ-ⓐⓗ

GENERAL INFORMATION

Climate in Latin America and Spain is diverse. Weather is largely affected by altitude and terrain.

SEASONS

Spring

La primavera

L@h PR€€-M@h-V€̆-R@h

Summer

El verano

€̆L V€̆-R@h-N①

Autumn

El otoño

€̆L ①-T①́N-Y①

Winter

El invierno

€̆L €€N-V€€-€̆́R-N①

THE DAYS

Monday
lunes
LOO-NēS

Tuesday
martes
Mah-TēS

Wednesday
miércoles
MEE-ēR-KO-LēS

Thursday
jueves
WHē-VēS

Friday
viernes
VEE-ēR-NēS

Saturday
sábado
Sah-Bah-DO

Sunday
domingo
DO-MEEN-GO

THE MONTHS

January	**February**
enero	febrero
ⓔ-Nⓔ-Ⓡⓞ	Fⓔ-BⓇⓔ-Ⓡⓞ
March	**April**
marzo	abril
MⓐⓗB-Sⓞ	ⓐⓗ-BⓇⒺL
May	**June**
mayo	junio
Mⓐⓗ-Yⓞ	Hⓞⓞ-NⒺ-ⓞ
July	**August**
julio	agosto
Hⓞⓞ-LⒺ-ⓞ	ⓐⓗ-Gⓞ S-Tⓞ
September	**October**
septiembre	octubre
Sⓔ P-TⒺ-ⓔM-BⓇⓔ	ⓞK-Tⓞⓞ-BⓇⓔ
November	**December**
noviembre	diciembre
Nⓞ-VⒺ-ⓔM-BⓇⓔ	DⒺ-SⒺ-ⓔM-BⓇⓔ

COLORS

Black	**White**
Negro	Blanco
Nⓔ-GRⓄ	BLⓐN-KⓄ

Blue	**Brown**
Azul	Café
ⓐ-Sⓞⓞ́L	Kⓐ-Fⓔ́

Gray	**Gold**
Gris	Oro
GRⓔⓔS	Ⓞ́-RⓄ

Orange	**Yellow**
Anaranjado	Amarillo
ⓐ-Nⓐ-Rⓐ́N-Hⓐ-DⓄ	ⓐ-Mⓐ-Rⓔⓔ́-YⓄ

Red	**Green**
Rojo	Verde
RⓄ́-HⓄ	Vⓔ́R-Dⓔ

Pink	**Purple**
Rosado	Morado
RⓄ-Sⓐ́-DⓄ	MⓄ-Rⓐ́-DⓄ

NUMBERS

0	**1**	**2**
Cero	Uno	Dos
S€-RO	∞-NO	DOS

3	**4**	**5**
Tres	Cuatro	Cinco
TR€S	KW@-TRO	S€N-KO

6	**7**	**8**
Seis	Siete	Ocho
S@S	S€-€-T€	O-CHO

9	**10**	**11**
Nueve	Diez	Once
NW€-V€	D€-€S	ON-S€

12	**13**	**14**
Doce	Trece	Catorce
DO-S€	TR€-S€	K@-TOR-S€

15	**16**	
Quince	Dieciséis	
K€N-S€	D€-€S-€-S@S	

17

Diecisiete

D€-€S-€-S€-€-T€

18

Dieciocho

DEE-ēS-EE-Ō-CHŌ

19	**20**
Diecinueve	Veinte
DEE-ēS-EE-NWē-Vē	VĀN-Tē

30	**40**
Treinta	Cuarenta
TRĀN-Tah	KWah-RēN-Tah

50	**60**
Cincuenta	Sesenta
SEEN-KWēN-Tah	Sē-SēN-Tah

70	**80**
Setenta	Ochenta
Sē-TēN-Tah	Ō-CHēN-Tah

90	**100**
Noventa	Cien
NŌ-VēN-Tah	SEE-ēN

1000	**1,000,000**
Mil	Millón
MEEL	MEE-YŌN

SPANISH VERBS

Verbs are the action words of any language. In Spanish there are three main types; **–ar**, **–er**, and **–ir**.

The foundation form for all verbs is called the infinitive. This is the form you will find in dictionaries. In English, we place "to" in front of the verb name to give us the infinitive; e.g., to speak. In Spanish. the infinitive is one word; **hablar**, and means by itself to speak, and (as in English) it does not change its form.

On the following pages you will see the present tense conjugation of the three regular verb groups: **–ar**, **–er**, and **–ir**. Conjugating a verb is what you do naturally in your own language: *I speak, he eats, they live*. A verb is called regular when it follows one of these three models: its basic form does not change, just the endings that correspond to the subject of the verb.

In your study of Spanish, you will come across irregular verbs and verbs with spelling changes. Their conjugation will require memorization. However, the Phrasemaker on page 128 will help you avoid this problem. First choose a form of want, then select an infinitive; 150 are provided in the following section. And because the infintive does not change, you don't need to worry about the conjugation of the verb or whether it is regular or irregular!

–AR VERB CONJUGATION

Find below the present tense conjugation for the regular **–AR** verb **hablar**, meaning **to speak**. The English equivalent is: *I speak* (or *I am speaking*), *you speak* (*you are speaking*), etc. For regular **–AR** verbs like this, drop the infinitive ending and add **-o**, **-as**, **-a**, **-amos**, **-áis** or **-an**.

I speak.

Yo hablo.

YO aB-LO

You speak. (informal)

Tu hablas.

Too aB-LaS

He speaks. / She speaks. / You speak. (formal)

El / Ella / Usted habla.

EL / E-Yah / ooS-TED aB-Lah

We speak.

Nosotros hablamos.

NO-SO-TROS aB-Lah-MOS

You speak. (plural)

Vosotros habláis.

VO-SO-TROS aB-LIS

They speak.

Ellos / Ellas / Ustedes hablan.

E-YOS / E-YahS / ooS-TE-DES aB-LahN

–ER VERB CONJUGATION

Find below the present tense conjugation for the regular
–ER verb **comer** meaning, **to eat**. The English equivalent
is: *I eat* (or *am eating*), *you eat* (*you are eating*), etc. For
regular –ER verbs like this, drop the infinitive ending
and add **-o**, **-es**, **-e**, **-emos**, **-éis** or **-an**.

I eat.

Yo com**o**.

YⓄ KⓄ-MⓄ

You eat. (informal)

Tu com**es**.

Tⓞⓞ KⓄ-Mⓔ S

He eats. / She eats. / You eat. (formal)

El / Ella / Usted com**e**.

ⓔL / ⓔ-Yⓐ / ⓞⓞS-TⓔD KⓄ-Mⓔ

We eat.

Nosotros com**emos**.

NⓄ-SⓄ-TⓡⓄS KⓄ-Mⓔ-MⓄS

You eat. (plural)

Vosotros com**éis**.

VⓄ-SⓄ-TⓡⓄS KⓄ-Mⓐ S

They eat.

Ellos / Ellas / Ustedes com**an**.

ⓔ-YⓄS / ⓔ-Yⓐ S / ⓞⓞS-TⓔD-ⓔS KⓄ-Mⓔ N

–IR VERB CONJUGATION

Find below the present tense conjugation for the regular
–IR verb **vivir** meaning **to live**. The English equivalent
is: *I live* (or *I am living*), *you live* (*you are living*), etc.
For regular **–IR** verbs like this, drop the infinitive ending
and add **-o**, **-es**, **-e**, **-imos**, **-ís** or **-en**.

I live.

Yo vivo.

YO VĒ-VO

You live. (informal)

Tu vives.

TOO VĒ-VĕS

He lives. / She lives. / You live. (formal)

El / Ella / Usted vive.

ĔL / Ĕ-Yah / OOS-TĔD VĒ-Vĕ

We live.

Nosotros vivimos.

NO-SŌ-TROS VĒ-VĒ-MOS

You live (plural)

Vosotros vivís.

VO-SŌ-TROS VĒ-VĒS

They live.

Ellos / Ellas / Ustedes viven.

Ĕ-YOS / Ĕ-YahS / OOS-TĔ-DĕS VĒ-VĕN

PHRASEMAKER

I want...

Yo quiero...

YO KEE-ĕ-RO...

It is easy to recognize Spanish verbs in their infinitive form because they always end in **-ar**, **-er**, or **-ir**!

You want...

Tú quieres... (informal)

TOO KEE-ĕ-RĕS...

Usted quiere... (formal)

OOS-TĕD KEE-ĕ-Rĕ...

He wants... ◀

▶ **to speak**

El quiere...

hablar

ĕL KEE-ĕ-Rĕ...

ahB-LahR

She wants... ◀

▶ **to eat**

Ella quiere...

comer

ĕ-Yah KEE-ĕ-Rĕ...

KO-MĕR

We want... ◀

▶ **to live**

Nosotros queremos..

vivir

NO-SO-TROS

VEE-VĕR

KEE-ĕR-MOS...

They want...

Ellos quieren...

ĕ-YOS KEE-ĕ-RĕN...

150 VERBS

Here are some essential verbs that will carry you a long way towards learning Spanish with the EPLS Vowel Symbol System!

to add

añadir

@N-Y@-D@R

to allow

permitir

P@R-M@-T@R

to answer

responder

R@S-P@N-D@R

to arrive

llegar

Y@-G@R

to ask

preguntar

PR@-G@N-T@R

to attack

atacar

@-T@-K@R

to attend

asistir

@-S@S-T@R

to bake (oven)

hornear

@R-N@-@R

to be (temporary)

estar

@S-T@R

to be (permanent)

ser

S@R

to be able

poder

P@-D@R

to beg

mendigar

M@N-D@-G@R

129

to begin

comenzar

KO-MEN-SahR

to believe

creer

KRE-ER

to break

romper

ROM-PER

to breathe

respirar

RES-PEE-RahR

to bring

llevar

YE-VahR

to build

construir

KON-STRoo-ER

to burn

quemar

KE-MahR

to buy

comprar

KOM-PRahR

to call

llamar

Yah-MahR

to cancel

cancelar

KahN-SEL-ahR

to carry

llevar

YE-VahR

to change

cambiar

KahM-BEE-ahR

to chew

masticar

MahS-TEE-KahR

to clean

limpiar

LEEM-PEE-ahR

to climb

subir

S⊙⊙-B𝐸𝐸R

to close

cerrar

S𝐸-RahR

to come

venir

V𝐸-N𝐸𝐸R

to cook

cocinar

K⊙-S𝐸𝐸-NahR

to count

contar

K⊙N-TahR

to convert

convertir

K⊙N-V𝐸-T𝐸𝐸R

to cry

llorar

Y⊙-RahR

to cut

cortar

K⊙R-TahR

to dance

bailar

BⒾ-LahR

to decide

decidir

D𝐸-S𝐸𝐸-D𝐸𝐸R

to depart

salir

Sah-L𝐸𝐸R

to desire

desear

D𝐸-S𝐸-ahR

disturb

molestar

M⊙-L𝐸S-TahR

to do

hacer

ah-S𝐸R

to drink
beber
B&ebar;-B&ebar;R

to drive
manejar
M&ah;-N&EE;-H&ah;R

to dry
secar
S&ebar;-K&ah;R

to earn
ganar
G&ah;-N&ah;R

to eat
comer
K&O;-M&ebar;R

to explain
explicar
&ebar;KS-PL&EE;-K&ah;R

to enjoy
disfrutar
D&EE;S-FR&oo;-T&ah;R

to enter
entrar
&ebar;N-TR&ah;R

to feel
sentir
S&ebar;N-T&EE;R

to fight
luchar
L&oo;-CH&ah;R

to fill
llenar
Y&ebar;-N&ah;R

to find
encontrar
&ebar;N-K&O;N-TR&ah;R

to finish
terminar
T&ebar;R-M&EE;-N&ah;R

to fix
fijar
F&EE;-H&ah;R

to fly	**to happen**
volar	pasar
VO-L@R	P@-S@R
to follow	**to have**
seguir	tener
Sē-Gēr	Tē-Nēr
to forgive	**to hear**
perdonar	escuchar
Pēr-DO-N@R	ēS-Koo-CH@R
to get	**to help**
obtener	ayudar
OB-Tē-Nēr	@-Yoo-D@R
to give	**to hide**
dar	ocultar
D@R	O-Kool-T@R
to go	**to hit** (fight)
ir	golpear
Ēr	GOL-Pē-@R
to greet	**to imagine**
saludar	imaginar
S@-Loo-D@R	ēē-M@-Hēē-N@R

to improve

mejorar

Mê-HO-RaB

to judge

juzgar

HοοS-GaB

to jump

saltar

SaL-TaB

to kiss

besar

Bê-SaB

to know

saber

Sa-BêB

to laugh

reír

Rê-EEB

to learn

aprender

a-PRêN-DêB

to leave

dejar

Dê-HaB

to lie (not the truth)

mentir

MêN-TêB

to lift

levantar

Lê-VaN-TaB

to like

gustar

GοοS-TaB

to listen

escuchar

êS-Kοο-CHaB

to live

vivir

VEE-VEEB

to look

mirar

MEE-RaB

to lose

perder

PĒR-DĒR

to love

amar

ah-MahR

to make

hacer

ah-SĒR

to measure

medir

MĒ-DEER

to miss

perder

PĒR-DĒR

to move

mover

MO-VĒR

to need

necesitar

NĒ-SĒ-SEE-TahR

to offer

ofrecer

O-FRĒ-SĒR

to open

abrir

ah-BRĒR

to order

ordenar

OR-DĒ-NahR

to pack

empacar

ĒM-Pah-KahR

to pass (object/time)

pasar

Pah-SahR

to pay (for)

pagar

Pah-GahR

to play

jugar

Hoo-GahR

to pretend

pretender

PRĕ-TĕN-DĕR

to print

imprimir

ĔM-PRĔ-MĔR

to promise

prometer

PRO-Mĕ-TĕR

to pronounce

pronunciar

PRO-NooN-SĔ-ahR

to push

empujar

ĔM-Poo-HahR

to put

poner

PO-NĕR

to quit

dejar

Dĕ-HahR

to read

leer

Lĕ-ĕR

to receive

recibir

Rĕ-SĔ-BĔR

to recomend

recomendar

Rĕ-KO-MĔN-DahR

to rent

alquilar

ahL-KĔ-LahR

remember

recordar

Rĕ-KOR-DahR

to rescue

rescatar

Rĕ-SKah-TahR

to rest

descansar

DĕS-KahN-SahR

to return (an item)
volver
VOL-VĕR

to run
correr
KO-RĕR

to say
decir
Dĕ-SEER

to see
ver
VĕR

to sell
vender
VĕN-DĕR

to show (display)
mostrar
MOS-TRahR

to shower
duchar
Doo-CHahR

to sign
firmar
FEER-MahR

to sing
cantar
KahN-TahR

to sit
sentar
SĕN-TahR

to sleep
dormir
DOR-MEER

to smoke
fumar
Foo-MahR

to smile
sonreír
SON-RA-EER

to speak
hablar
ah-BLahR

to spell

deletrear

D(ē)-L(ah)-TR(ē)-(ah)R

to spend (time)

pasar

P(ah)-S(ah)R

to start / to begin

empezar

(ē)M-P(ē)-S(ah)R

to stay

permanecer

P(ē)R-M(ah)-N(ē)-S(ē)R

to stop

parar

P(ah)-R(ah)R

to study

estudiar

(ē)S-T(oo)-D(ēē)-(ah)R

to succeed (achieve)

lograr

L(ō)-GR(ah)R

to swim

nadar

N(ah)-D(ah)R

to take

tomar

T(ō)-M(ah)R

to talk

hablar

(ah)-BL(ah)R

to teach

enseñar

(ē)N-S(ē)N-Y(ah)R

to tell

decir

D(ē)-S(EE)R

to touch (play instrument)

tocar

T(ō)-K(ah)R

to think

pensar

P(ē)N-S(ah)R

to travel
viajar
V(EE)-(ah)-H(ah)R

to try (attempt)
tratar
TR(ah)-T(ah)R

to understand
comprender
K(O)M-PR(e)N-D(e)R

to use
usar
(oo)-S(ah)R

to visit
visitar
V(EE)-S(EE)-T(ah)R

to wait
esperar
(e)S-P(e)-R(ah)R

to walk
caminar
K(ah)-M(EE)-N(ah)R

to want
querer
K(e)-R(e)R

to wash
lavar
L(ah)-V(ah)R

to watch (look)
ver
V(e)R

to win
ganar
G(ah)-N(ah)R

to work
trabajar
TR(ah)-B(ah)-H(ah)R

to worry
preocupar
PR(e)-(O)-K(oo)-P(ah)R

to write
escribir
(e)S-KR(EE)-B(EE)R

DICTIONARY

Each English entry is followed by the Spanish word and the EPLS transliteration. Gender of nouns is indicated by (m) for masculine and (f) for feminine.

Plural is indicated by (/pl). Adjectives are shown in their masculine form, as common practice dictates. Adjectives and some nouns that end in **o** or **os** can usually be changed to feminine by changing the ending to **a** or **as**. Verbs appear in infinitive form, indicated by (to).

A

a, an un (m) / una (f) ⓞⓞN / ⓞⓞ-Nⓐ

a lot mucho Mⓞⓞ-CHⓞ

able (to be) poder Pⓞ-THⓔⓇ

above sobre Sⓞ-BRⓔ

accident accidente (m) ⓐK-Sⓔⓔ-Dⓔ-N-Tⓔ

accommodation alojamiento (m)
  ⓐ-Lⓞ-Hⓐ-Mⓔⓔ-ⓔN-Tⓞ

account cuenta (f) KWⓔN-Tⓐ

address dirección (f) Dⓔⓔ-Rⓔ-K-Sⓔⓔ-ⓞN

admission admisión (f) ⓐD-Mⓔⓔ-Sⓔⓔ-ⓞN

afraid tener miedo TⓔN-ⓔⓇ Mⓔⓔ-ⓔ-THⓞ

after después DⓔS-PWⓔS

afternoon tarde (f) TAR-DE

air-conditioning aire acondicionado (m)
I-RE ah-KON-DEE-SEE-O-NAH-DO

aircraft avión (m) ah-VEE-ON

airline línea aérea (f) LEE-NE-ah ah-E-RE-ah

airport aeropuerto (m) ah-E-RO-PWER-TO

aisle pasillo (m) PAH-SEE-YO

all todo TO-THO

almost casi KAH-SEE

alone solo SO-LO

also también TAHM-BEE-EN

always siempre SEE-EM-PRE

ambulance ambulancia (f) AHM-Boo-LAhN-SEE-ah

American americano (m) ah-ME-REE-KAH-NO
americana (f) ah-ME-REE-KAH-Nah

and y EE

another otro O-TRO

anything algo AhL-GO

apartment apartamento (m) ah-PAhR-TAh-MEN-TO

appetizers entremeses (m/pl) EN-TRE-ME-SES

apple manzana (f) MAhN-SAh-Nah

appointment cita (f) SEE-Tah

April abril (m) ah-BREEL

arrival llegada (f) YĒ-Gah-Dah

arrive (to) llegar YĒ-GahR

ashtray cenicero SĒ-NEE-SĒ-RO

aspirin aspirina (f) ah-SPEE-REE-Nah

attention ¡atención! ah-TĒN-SEE-ON

August agosto (m) ah-GOS-TO

Australia Australia ow-STRA-LEE-uh

Australian Australiano (m) ow-STRA-LEE-uh-NO
Australiana (f) ow-STRA-LEE-uh-Nah

author autor (m) ow-TOR

automobile automóvil (m) ow-TO-MO-VEEL

autumn otoño (m) O-TON-YO

avenue avenida (f) ah-VĒN-EE-Dah

awful horrible O-REE-BLĒ

B

baby bebé (m) BĒ-BĒ
babysitter niñera (f) NEEN-YĒ-Rah
bacon tocino (m) TO-SEE-NO

bad malo Mah-LO

bag maleta (f) Mah-LE-Tah

baggage equipaje (m) e-KEE-Pai-He

baked al horno ahL OR-NO

bakery panadería (f) Pah-Nah-DE-REE-ah

banana plátano (m) PLah-Tah-NO

Band-Aid curita (f) Koo-REE-Tah

bank banco (m) BahN-KO

barbershop peluquería (f) Pe-Loo-Ke-REE-ah

bartender cantinero (m) KahN-TEE-NE-RO

bath baño (m) BahN-YO

bathing suit traje de baño (m)
    TRah-He De BahN-YO

bathroom baño (m) BahN-YO

battery batería (f) / pila (f) Bah-TE-REE-ah / PEE-Lah

beach playa (f) PLah-Yah

beautiful bello BE-YO

beauty shop salón de belleza (m)
    Sah-LON De Be-Ye-Sah

bed cama (f) Kah-Mah

beef carne de res (f) KahR-Ne De ReS

beer cerveza (f) SeR-Ve-Sah

bellman botones (m) BO-TO-NeS

belt cinturón (m) SeeN-Too-RON

big grande GRahN-De

bill cuenta (f) KWeN-Tah

black negro Ne-GRO

blanket cobija (f) KO-Bee-Hah
    manta (f) (Spain) MahN-Tah

blue azul ah-SooL

boat barco (m) BahR-KO

book libro (m) Lee-BRO

bookstore librería (f) Lee-BRe-Ree-ah

border frontera (f) FRON-Te-Rah

boy muchacho (m) Moo-CHah-CHO

bracelet pulsera (f) PooL-Se-Rah

brake freno (m) FRe-NO

bread pan (m) PahN

breakfast desayuno (m) De-Sah-Yoo-NO

broiled a la parrilla ah Lah Pah-Ree-Yah

brown café Kah-Fe

brush cepillo (m) Se-Pee-YO

building edificio (m) ⓔ-Dⓔⓔ-Fⓔⓔ-Sⓔⓔ-Ⓞ

bus autobús (m) ⓦ-TⓄ-Bⓞⓞ'S

bus station estación de autobuses (f)
ⓔ-STⓐⓗ-Sⓔⓔ-ⓄN Dⓔ ⓦ-TⓄ-Bⓞⓞ-Sⓔⓢ

bus stop parada de autobuses (f)
Pⓐⓗ-Bⓐⓗ-Dⓐⓗ Dⓔ ⓦ-TⓄ-Bⓞⓞ-Sⓔⓢ

business negocios (m) Nⓔ-GⓄ-Sⓔⓔ-ⓄS

butter mantequilla (f) MⓐⓗN-Tⓔ-Kⓔⓔ-Yⓐⓗ

buy (to) comprar KⓄM-PBⓐⓗB

C

cab taxi (m) TⓐⓗK-Sⓔⓔ

call (to) llamar Yⓐⓗ-MⓐⓗB

camera cámara (f) Kⓐⓗ-Mⓐⓗ-Bⓐⓗ

Canada Canadá Kⓐⓗ-Nⓐⓗ-Dⓐⓗ

Canadian el canadiense (m) ⓔL Kⓐⓗ-Nⓐⓗ-Dⓔⓔ-ⓔN-Sⓔ
    (f) la canadiense Lⓐⓗ Kⓐⓗ-Nⓐⓗ-Dⓔⓔ-ⓔN-Sⓔ

candy dulce (m) DⓞⓞL-Sⓔ

car carro (m) / coche (m) / automóvil (m)
    Kⓐⓗ-BⓄ / KⓄ-CHⓔ / ⓦ-TⓄ-MⓄ-VⓔL

carrot zanahoria (f) Sⓐⓗ-NⓄ-Bⓔⓔ-ⓐⓗ

castle castillo (m) Kⓐⓗ-STⓔⓔ-YⓄ

cathedral catedral (f)   Kah-Tē-DRahL

celebration celebración (f)   Sē-Lē-BRah-Sē-ON

center centro   Sēn-TRO

cereal cereal (m)   Sē-Rē-ahL

chair silla (f)   Sēē-Yah

champagne champaña (m)   CHahM-Pahn-Yah

change (to) cambiar   KahM-Bēē-ahR

change (money) cambio (m)   KahM-Bēē-O

cheap barato   Bah-Rah-TO

check (restaurant bill) cheque (m)   CHē-Kē

cheers! ¡salud!   Sah-LooD

cheese queso (m)   Kē-SO

chicken pollo (m)   PO-YO

child niño (m) / niña (f)   Nēēn-YO / Nēēn-Yah

chocolate chocolate   CHO-KO-Lah-Tē

church iglesia (f)   EE-GLē-Sēē-ah

cigar puro (m)   Poo-RO

cigarette cigarrillo (m)   Sēē-Gah-Rēē-YO

city ciudad (f)   Sēē-oo-DahD

clean limpio   LēēM-Pēē-O

close (to) cerrar S℮-R@R

closed cerrado S℮-R@-DO

clothes ropa (f) RO-P@

cocktail cóctel (m) KOK-T℮L

coffee café (m) K@-F℮

cold (temperature) frío FR℮-O

comb peine (m) P@-N℮

come (to) venir V℮-N℮R

company compañía (f) KOM-P@N-Y℮-@

computer computadora (f) KOM-P∞-T@-DO-R@
ordenador (m) (Spain) OR-D℮-N@-DOR

concert concierto (m) KON-S℮-℮R-TO

condom profiláctico (m) PRO-F℮-L@K-T℮-KO

conference conferencia (f) KON-F℮-R℮N-S℮-@

conference room salón de conferencias (m)
S@-LON D℮ KON-F℮-R℮N-S℮-@S

congratulations felicitaciones (f/pl)
F℮-L℮-S℮-T@-S℮-O-N℮S

copy machine máquina para hacer copias (f)
M@-K℮-N@ P@-R@ @-S℮R KO-P℮-@S
Xerox (m) Z℮-R@KS

corn maíz (m)   Mah-ÉS

cough syrup calmante de la tos (m)
    KahL-MahN-Tē Dē Lah TOS

cover charge cargo mínimo (m)
    KahR-GO Mēē-Nēē-MO

crab cangrejo (m)   KahN-GRē-HO

cream crema (f)   KRē-Mah

credit card tarjeta de crédito (f)
    TahR-Hē-Tah Dē KRē-Dēē-TO

cup taza (f)   Tah-Sah

customs aduana (f)   ah-DWah-Nah

D

dance (to) bailar Bɪ-LahR

dangerous peligroso Pē-Lēē-GRO-SO

date (calendar) fecha (f) Fē-CHah

day día (m) Dēē-ah

December diciembre (m)   Dēē-Sēē-ēM-BRē

delicious delicioso Dē-Lēē-Sēē-O-SO

delighted encantado ēN-KahN-Tah-DO

dentist dentista (m) DēN-Tēēs-Tah

deodorant desodorante (m) Dē-SO-DO-RahN-Tē

department store almacén (m) ah-L-Mah-SON

departure salida (f) Sah-L-EE-Dah

dessert postre (m) POS-TRE

detour desviación (f) DES-V-EE-ah-SEE-ON

diabetic diabético (m) DEE-ah-BE-TEE-KO

diarrhea diarrea (f) DEE-ah-RE-ah

dictionary diccionario (m) DEEK-SEE-O-Nah-REE-O

dinner cena (f) SE-Nah

dining room comedor (m) KO-ME-DOR

direction dirección (f) DEE-REK-SEE-ON

dirty sucio SOO-SEE-O

disabled inválido (m) EEN-Vah-LEE-DO

discount descuento (m) DES-KWON-TO
    rebaja (f) RE-Bah-Hah

distance distancia (f) DEES-Tah'N-SEE-ah

doctor médico (m) ME-DEE-KO

document documento (m) DO-KOO-MEN-TO

dollar dólar (m) DO-Lah-R

down abajo ah-Bah-HO

downtown el centro EL SEN-TRO

dress vestido (m) VES-TEE-DO

drink (to) beber　Bĕ-BĕR

drive (to) manejar　Mah-Nĕ-HahR

drugstore farmacia (f)　FahR-Mah-SEE-ah

dry cleaner tintorería (f)　TEEN-TO-Rĕ-REE-ah

duck pato (m)　Pah-TO

E

ear oreja (f) / oído (m)　O-Rĕ-Hah　/　O-EE-THO

ear drops gotas para los oídos (f/pl)
　GO-TahS Pah-Rah LOS O-EE-DOS

early temprano　TĕM-PRah-NO

east este (m)　ĕS-Tĕ

easy fácil　Fah-SEEL

eat (to) comer　KO-MĕR

egg huevo (m)　Wĕ-VO

eggs (fried) huevos fritos (m/pl)
　Wĕ-VOS FREE-TOS

eggs (scrambled) huevos revueltos (m/pl)
　Wĕ-VOS Rĕ-VWĕL-TOS

electricity electricidad (f)　ĕ-LĕK-TREE-SEE-DahD

elevator ascensor (m)　ah-SĕN-SOR

embassy embajada (f)　ĕM-Bah-Hah-Dah

emergency emergencia (f) ĕ-MĔR-HĔN-SĒ-ah

England Inglaterra (f) ĔN-GLah-TĔ-Rah

English inglés (m) ĔN-GLĕS

enough! ¡Basta! Bah'S-Tah

entrance entrada (f) ĕN-TRah-Dah

envelope sobre (m) SŌ-BRĕ

evening tarde (f) Tah'R-Dĕ

everything todo TŌ-DŌ

excellent excelente ĕK-Sĕ-LĔN-Tĕ

excuse me perdón PĕR-DŌN

exit salida (f) Sah-LĒ-Dah

expensive caro Kah'-RŌ

eye ojo (m) Ō-HŌ

eyedrops gotas para los ojos (f/pl)
    GŌ-Tah'S Pah'-Rah LŌS Ō-HŌS

F

face cara (f) Kah'-Rah

far lejos Lĕ'-HŌS

fare billete (m) Bĕ-Yĕ'-Tĕ

fast rápido Rah'-Pĕ-DŌ

fax, fax machine fax (m) Fah'KS

February febrero (m) Fĕ-BRĕ-RO

few poco PO-KO

film (movie) película (f) Pĕ-Lĕ-Koo-Lah

film (camera) rollo de cámara (m)
     RO-YO Dĕ Kah-Mah-Rah

fine muy bien MWĕ Bĕ-ĕN

finger dedo (m) Dĕ-THO

fire fuego (m) FWĕ-GO

fire! ¡incendio! ĕN-Sĕ̈N-Dĕ-O

fire extinguisher extintor (m) ĕKS-Tĕ̈N-TOR

first primero PRĕ-Mĕ-RO

fish pescado (m) Pĕ̈S-Kah-DO

flight vuelo (m) VWĕ-LO

florist shop florería (f) FLO-Rĕ-Rĕ-ah

flower flor (f) FLOR

food comida (f) KO-Mĕ-Dah

foot pie (m) Pĕ-ĕ

fork tenedor (m) Tĕ-Nĕ-DOR

french fries papas fritas (f/pl) Pah-PahS FRĕ-TahS
     patatas fritas (Spain) Pah-Tah-TahS FRĕ-TahS

fresh fresco FRĕ̈S-KO

Friday viernes (m)   Vẽẽ-ẽR-NẽS

fried frito   FRẽẽ-TⓄ

friend amigo (m) / amiga (f)
Ⓐ-Mẽẽ-GⓄ / Ⓐ-Mẽẽ-GⒶ

fruit fruta (f)   FRⓅⓅ-TⒶ

funny gracioso   GRⒶ-Sẽẽ-Ⓞ-SⓄ

G

gas station gasolinera (f)   GⒶ-SⓄ-Lẽẽ-Nẽ-RⒶ

gasoline petróleo (m)   Pẽ-TRⓄ-Lẽ-Ⓞ

gate puerta (f)   PWẽR-TⒶ

gentleman caballero (m)   KⒶ-BⒶ-Yẽ-RⓄ

gift regalo (m)   Rẽ-GⒶ-LⓄ

girl muchacha (f)   MⓅⓅ-CHⒶ-CHⒶ

glass (drinking) vaso (m)   VⒶ-SⓄ

glasses (eye) lentes (m/pl)   LẽN-TẽS

glove guante (m)   GWⒶN-Tẽ

go vaya   VⒶ-YⒶ

gold oro (m)   Ⓞ-RⓄ

golf golf (m)   GⓄLF

golf course campo de golf (m)
KⒶM-PⓄ Dẽ GⓄLF

good bueno BWĒ-NO

good-bye adiós ah-DEE-OS

goose ganso (m) GahN-SO

grapes uvas (f) oo-VahS

grateful agradecido ah-GRah-DĒ-SĒ-DO

gray gris GREES

green verde VĒR-DĒ

grocery store tienda de comestibles (f)
    TEE-ĒN-Dah DĒ KO-MĒS-TEE-BLĒS

group grupo (m) GRoo-PO

guide guía (m) GEE-ah

H

hair cabello (m) Kah-BĒ-YO

hairbrush cepillo (m) SĒ-PEE-YO

haircut corte de pelo (m) KOR-TĒ DĒ PĒ-LO

ham jamón Hah-MON

hamburger hamburguesa (f) ahM-Boo R-GĒ-Sah

hand la mano (f) Lah Mah-NO

happy feliz FĒ-LEES

have (to) tener TĒN-ĒR

he él ＥL

head cabeza (f) KＡ-BＥ-SＡ

headache dolor de cabeza (m)
DO-LOB Dè CＡ-BＥ-SＡ

health club gimnasio (m) HＥM-NＡ-SＥ-O
club (m) KLＯＯB

heart corazón (m) KO-BＡ-SON

heart condition sufro del corazón (m)
SＯＯ-FBO DＥL KO-BＡ-SON

heat calefacción (f) KＡ-LＥ-FＡK-SＥ-ON

hello hola O-LＡ

help! ¡socorro! SO-KO-BO

here aquí Ａ-KＥ

holiday día feriado (m) DＥ-Ａ FＥ-BＥ-Ａ-DO

hospital hospital (m) OS-PＥ-TＡL

hot dog hot dog (m) HＡT DＡG

hotel hotel (m) O-TＥL

hour hora (f) O-BＡ

how ¿cómo? KO-MO

hurry up! ¡apúrese! Ａ-PＯＯ-BＥ-SＥ

husband esposo ＥS-PO-SO

I

I yo   YO

ice hielo (m)   YÉ-LO

ice cream nieve (f)   NEE-É-VÉ
   helado (m) (Spain)   É-LAH-DO

ice cubes cubitos de hielo (m/pl)
   KOO-BEE-TOS DÉ YÉ-LO

ill enfermo   ÉN-FÉR-MO

important importante   EEM-POR-TAHN-TÉ

indigestion indigestión (f)   EEN-DEE-HÉS-TÉ-YON

information información (f)   EEN-FOR-MAH-SEE-ON

inn posada (f)   PO-SAH-DAH

interpreter intérprete (m)   EEN-TÉR-PRÉ-TÉ

J

jacket chaqueta (f)   CHAH-KÉ-TAH

jam mermelada (f)   MÉR-MÉ-LAH-DAH

January enero (m)   É-NÉ-RO

jewelry joyas (f)   HOY-AHS

jewelry store joyería (f)   Hoy-ē-RĒE-ah

job trabajo (m)   TRah-Bah-HO

juice jugo (m)   Hoo-GO

July julio (m)   Hoo-LĒE-O

June junio (m)   Hoo-NĒE-O

K

ketchup ketchup (m)   Kē-CHooP

key llave (f)   Yah-Vē

kiss beso (m)   Bē-SO

knife cuchillo (m)   Koo-CHĒE-YO

L

ladies' restroom servicios de señoras (m/pl)
   SēR-VĒE-SĒE-OS Dē SēN-YO-Rah S

lady dama (f)   Dah-Mah

lamb cordero (m)   KOR-Dē-RO

language idioma (m)   ĒE-DĒE-O-Mah

large grande   GRah N-Dē

late tarde   Tah R-Dē

laundry lavandería (f)   Lah-Vah N-Dē-RĒE-ah

lawyer abogado (m)   ah-BO-Gah-DO

left (direction) izquierda ⒺS-KⒺ-ⒺR-Dⓐʰ

leg pierna (f) PⒺ-ⒺR-Nⓐʰ

lemon limón (m) LⒺ-MⓄN

less menos MⒺ-NⓄS

letter carta (f) KⓐʰR-Tⓐʰ

lettuce lechuga (f) LⒺ-CHⓄⓄ-Gⓐʰ

light luz (f) LⓄⓄS

like (I) me gusta MⒺ GⓄⓄS-Tⓐʰ

lip labio (m) Lⓐʰ-BⒺ-Ⓞ

lipstick pintura de labios (f)
    PⒺN-TⓄⓄ-Rⓐʰ DⒺ Lⓐʰ-BⒺ-ⓄS

little (amount) poquito PⓄ-KⒺ-TⓄ

little (size) pequeño PⒺ-KⒺN-YⓄ

live (to) vivir VⒺ-VⒺR

lobster langosta (f) LⓐʰN-GⓄS-Tⓐʰ

long largo LⓐʰR-GⓄ

lost perdido PⒺR-DⒺ-DⓄ

love amor (m) ⓐʰ-MⓄR

luck suerte (f) SWⒺR-TⒺ

luggage equipaje (m) Ⓔ-KⒺ-Pⓐʰ-HⒺ

lunch almuerzo (m) ⓐʰL-MWⒺR-SⓄ

M

maid camarera (f) K@h-M@h-R@-R@h

mail correo (m) K⊙-R@-⊙

makeup maquillaje (m) M@h-K@-Y@h-H@

man hombre (m) ⊙M-BR@

manager gerente (m) H@-R@N-T@

map mapa (m) M@h-P@h

March marzo (m) M@hR-S⊙

market mercado (m) M@R-K@h-D⊙

match (light) cerillo (m), fósforo (m)
S@-R@-Y⊙ / F⊙S-F⊙-R⊙

May mayo (m) M@h-Y⊙

mayonnaise mayonesa (f) M@h-Y⊙-N@-S@h

meal comida (f) K⊙-M@-D@h

meat carne (f) K@hR-N@

mechanic mecánico (m) M@-K@h-N@-K⊙

medicine medicina (f) M@-D@-S@-N@h

meeting reunión (f) R@-oo-N@-⊙N

mens' restroom servicios de señores (m/pl)
S@R-V@-S@-⊙S D@ S@N-Y⊙-R@S

menu menú (m) M@-N◎

message recado (m)　RĒ-Kah-DO

milk leche (f)　LĒ-CHĒ

mineral water agua mineral (m)
　ah-GWah　MĒE-NĒ-Rahl

minute minuto (m)　MĒE-Noo-TO

Miss señorita (f)　SĒN-YO-RĒE-Tah

mistake error (f)　ĒE-ROR

misunderstanding equivocación (f)
　ĒE-KĒE-VO-Kah-SĒE-ON

moment momento (m)　MO-MĒN-TO

Monday lunes (m)　Loo-NĒS

money dinero (m)　DĒE-NĒ-RO

month mes (m)　MĒS

monument monumento (m)　MO-No-MĒN-TO

more más　MahS

morning mañana (f)　Mah-Yah-Nah

mosque mezquita (f)　MĒS-KĒE-Tah

mother madre (f)　Mah-DRĒ

mountain montaña (f)　MON-Tah-Yah

movies cine (m)　SĒE-NĒ

Mr. señor (m)　SĒN-YOR

Mrs. señora (f)　SĒN-YO-Rah

much (too) demasiado Dⓔ-Mⓐⓗ-SⒺⒺ-ⓐⓗ-DⓄ

museum museo (m) Mⓞⓞ-Sⓔ́-Ⓞ

mushrooms hongos (m/pl) ⓄN-GⓄS

music música (f) Mⓞⓞ-SⒺⒺ-Kⓐⓗ

mustard mostaza (f) MⓄS-Tⓐⓗ-Sⓐⓗ

N

nail polish esmalte para uñas (m)
ⓔS-MⓐⓗL-Tⓔ Pⓐⓗ-Rⓐⓗ ⓞⓞN-YⓐⓗS

name nombre (m) NⓄM-BRⓔ

napkin servilleta (f) Sⓔ̇R-VⒺⒺ-Yⓔ́-Tⓐⓗ

napkins (sanitary) almohadillas higiénicas (f)
ⓐⓗL-MⓄ-Hⓐⓗ-DⒺⒺ-YⓐⓗS ⒺⒺ-HⒺⒺ-ⓔ-NⒺⒺ-KⓐⓗS

near cerca Sⓔ̇R-Kⓐⓗ

neck cuello (m) KWⓔ́-YⓄ

need (I) necesito Nⓔ́-Sⓔ́-SⒺⒺ-TⓄ

never nunca NⓞⓞN-Kⓐⓗ

newspaper periódico (m) Pⓔ́-RⒺⒺ-Ⓞ́-DⒺⒺ-KⓄ

news stand quiosco de periódicos (m)
KⒺⒺ-Ⓞ́S-KⓄ Dⓔ́ Pⓔ́-RⒺⒺ-Ⓞ́-DⒺⒺ-KⓄS

night noche (f)   NO-CHe

nightclub cabaret (m)   Kah-Bah-ReT

no no   NO

no smoking no fumar   NO Foo-Mah'R

noon mediodía (m)   Me-Dee-O-Dee-ah

north norte (m)   NOR-Te

notary notario (m)   NO-Tah-Ree-O

November noviembre (m)   NO-Vee-eM-BRe

now ahora   ah-O-Rah

number número (m)   Noo-Me-RO

nurse enfermera (f)   eN-FeR-Me-Rah

O

occupied ocupado   O-Koo-Pah-DO

ocean océano   O-Se-ah-NO

October octubre (m)   OK-Too-BRe

officer oficial (m)   O-Fee-See-ahL

oil aceite (m)   ah-SA-Te

omelet tortilla de huevos (f)
   TOR-Tee-Yah De We-VOS

one-way (traffic) una vía   oo-Nah Vee-ah

onion cebolla (f)   Se-BO-Yah

open (to) abrir ⓐ-BRⒺⒷ

opera ópera (f) Ⓞ-PⒺ-Rⓐ

operator operadora (f) Ⓞ-PⒺ-Rⓐ-DⓄR-ⓐ

optician optometrista (m) ⓄP-TⓄ-MⒺ-TRⒺⓈ-Tⓐ

orange (color) anaranjado ⓐ-Nⓐ-Rⓐ-Nⓐ-Hⓐ-DⓄ

orange (fruit) naranja (f) Nⓐ-Rⓐ-Nⓐ-Hⓐ

order (to) ordenar ⓄR-DⒺ-Nⓐ-R

original original Ⓞ-RⒺ-HⒺ-Nⓐ-L

owner dueño (m) DWⒺ-N-YⓄ

oyster ostra (f) ⓄⓈ-TRⓐ

P

package paquete (m) Pⓐ-KⒺ-TⒺ

paid pagado Pⓐ-Gⓐ-DⓄ

pain dolor (m) DⓄ-LⓄR

painting pintura (f) PⒺN-TⓄⓄ-Rⓐ

pantyhose pantimedias (f/pl)
Pⓐ-N-TⒺ-MⒺ-DⒺ-ⓐⓈ

paper papel (m) Pⓐ-PⒺL

partner (business) socio (m) SⓄ-SⒺ-Ⓞ

party fiesta (f) FⒺ-ⒺⓈ-Tⓐ

passenger pasajero (m)　P@h-S@h-H@-R◎

passport pasaporte (m)　P@h-S@h-P◎B-T@

pasta pasta (f)　P@S-T@h

pastry pastel (m)　P@h-ST@L

pen pluma (f)　PL◉-M@h

pencil lápiz (m)　L@-P@S

pepper pimienta (f)　P@-M@-@N-T@h

perfume perfume (m)　P@B-F◉-M@

person persona (f)　P@B-S◎-N@h

person to person personal　P@B-S◎-N@L

pharmacist farmacéutico (m)　F@hB-M@h-S◉-T@-K◎

pharmacy farmacia (f)　F@hB-M@h-S@-@h

phone book guía telefónica (f)
　G@-@h　T@-L@-F◎-N@-K@h

photo foto (f)　F◎-T◎

photographer fotógrafo (m)　F◎-T◎-GB@h-F◎

pie pastel de (follow with name of filling)
　P@h-ST@L　D@

pillow almohada (f)　@L-M◎-@h-D@h

pink rosado　B◎-S@h-D◎

pizza pizza (f) PEET-Sah or PEE-Sah

plastic plástico (m) PLahS-TEE-KO

plate plato (m) PLah-TO

please por favor POR Fah-VOR

pleasure placer (m) PLah-SeR

police policía (f) PO-LEE-SEE-ah

police station comisaría (f) KO-MEE-Sah-REE-ah

pork carne de puerco (f) KahR-Ne De PWeR-KO

porter maletero (m) Mah-Le-Te-RO

post office correo (m) KO-Re-O

postcard tarjeta postal (f) TahR-He-Tah POS-TahL

potato papa (f) / patata (f) (Spain)
Pah-Pah / Pah-Tah-Tah

pregnant embarazada eM-Bah-Rah-Sah-Dah

prescription receta (f) Re-Se-Tah

price precio (m) PRe-SEE-O

problem problema (m) PRO-BLe-Mah

profession profesión (f) PRO-Fe-SEE-ON

public público POOB-LEE-KO

public telephone teléfono público (m)
Te-Le-FO-NO POOB-LEE-KO

purified purificada Poo-REE-FEE-Cah-Dah

purple morado MO-Rah-DO

purse bolsa (f) BOL-Sah

Q

quality calidad (f) Kah-LEE-DahD

question pregunta (f) PRe-GooN-Tah

quickly rápido Rah-PEE-DO

quiet callado Kah-Yah-DO

quiet! (be) ¡silencio! SEE-LeN-SEE-O

R

radio radio (f) Rah-DEE-O

railroad ferrocarril (m) Fe-RO-Kah-REEL

rain lluvia (f) Yoo-VEE-ah

raincoat impermeable (m)
  EEM-PeR-Me-ah-BLe

ramp rampa (f) RahM-Pah

rare (cooked) poco cocida PO-KO KO-SEE-Dah

razor blades hojas de afeitar (f/pl)
  O-Hah S De ah-Fe-TahR

ready listo (m) / lista (f) LEES-TO / LEES-Tah

receipt recibo (m) RĒ-SĒ-BO

recommend (to) recomendar RĒ-KO-MĒN-DāR

red rojo RŌ-HO

repeat! ¡repita! RĒ-PĒ-Tah

reservation reserva (f) / reservación (f)
 RĒ-SēR-Vah / RĒ-SēR-Vah-SĒ-ŌN

restaurant restaurante (m) RēS-Tow-RahN-Tē

return devolver Dē-VOL-VēR

rice arroz (m) ah-RŌS

rich rico RĒ-KO

right (correct) correcto KO-Rēk-TO

right (direction) derecha Dē-Rē-CHah

road camino (m) Kah-MĒ-NO

room cuarto (m) KWahR-TO

round trip ida y vuelta Ē-Dah Ē VWēL-Tah

S

safe (in a hotel) caja fuerte (f)
 Kah-Hah FWēR-Tē

salad ensalada (f) ēN-Sah-Lah-Dah

sale venta (f) VēN-Tah

salmon salmón (m) S@L-M⊙N

salt sal (f) S@L

sandwich torta (f) T⊙R-T@
   bocadillo (m) (Spain) B⊙-K@-D㏑-Y⊙

Saturday sábado (m) S@-B@-D⊙

scissors tijeras (f/pl) T㏑-H㋍-R@S

sculpture escultura (f) ㋍S-K⊚L-T⊚-R@

seafood mariscos (m/pl) M@-R㏑S-K⊙S

season estación (f) ㋍S-T@-S㏑-⊙N

seat asiento (m) @-S㏑-㋍N-T⊙

secretary secretaria (f) S㋍-KR㋍-T@-R㏑-@

section sección (f) S㋍K-S㏑-⊙N

September septiembre (m) S㋍P-T㏑-㋍M-BR㋍

service servicio (m) S㋍R-V㏑-S㏑-⊙

several varios V@-R㏑-⊙S

shampoo champú (m) CH@M-P⊚

sheets (bed) sábanas (f/pl) S@-B@-N@S

shirt camisa (f) K@-M㏑-S@

shoe zapato (m) S@-P@-T⊙

shoe store zapatería (f) S@-P@-T㋍-R㏑-@

shopping center centro comercial (m)
   S㋍N-TR⊙ K⊙-M㋍R-S㏑-@L

shower ducha (f) DOO-CHah

shrimp camarones (m/pl) Kah-Mah-ROH-NeS

sick enfermo eN-FeR-MO

sign (display) letrero (m) Le-TRe-RO

signature firma (f) FeeR-Mah

silence silencio See-Lee N-See-O

single solo SO-LO

sir señor (m) SeN-YOR

sister hermana (f) eR-Mah-Nah

size tamaño (m) Tah-Mah N-YO

skin piel (f) Pee-eL

skirt falda (f) FahL-Dah

sleeve manga (f) MahN-Gah

slowly despacio De-SPah-See-O

small pequeño Pe-Ke N-YO

smoke (to) fumar FOO-MahR

soap jabón (m) Hah-BON

socks calcetas (f/pl) / calcetines (m/pl)
KahL-Se-TahS / KahL-Se-Tee-NeS

some unos (m/pl), unas (f/pl) OO-NOS / OO-NahS
algunos / algunas (with numbers)
ahL-GOO-NOS / ahL-GOO-NahS

something algo ⓐⓗL-GⓄ

sometimes algunas veces ⓐⓗL-GⓄⓞ-NⓐⓗS Vⓔ-SⓔS

soon pronto PⓇⓄN-TⓄ

sorry (I am) lo siento LⓄ Sⓔⓔ-ⓔ́N-TⓄ

soup sopa (f) / caldo (m) SⓄ-Pⓐⓗ / KⓐⓗL-DⓄ

south sur (m) SⓄⓞⓇ

souvenir recuerdo (m) Ⓡⓔ-KWⓔⓇ-DⓄ

Spanish español (m) ⓔS-PⓐⓗN-YⓄL

special especial ⓔ-SPⓔ-Sⓔⓔ-ⓐⓗL

speed velocidad (f) Vⓔ-LⓄ-Sⓔⓔ-DⓐⓗD

spoon cuchara (f) Kⓞⓞ-CHⓐⓗ-Ⓡⓐⓗ

sport deporte (m) Dⓔ-PⓄⓇ-Tⓔ

spring (season) primavera (f) PⓇⓔⓔ-Mⓐⓗ-Vⓔ-Ⓡⓐⓗ

stairs escalera (f) ⓔS-Kⓐⓗ-Lⓔ́-Ⓡⓐⓗ

stamp sello (m) / timbre (m) Sⓔ́-YⓄ / TⓔⓔM-BⓇⓔ

station estación ⓔS-Tⓐⓗ-Sⓔⓔ-ⓄN

steak bistec (m) Bⓔⓔ-STⓔ́K

steamed cocido a vapor KⓄ-Sⓔⓔ́-DⓄ ⓐⓗ Vⓐⓗ-PⓄⓇ

stop pare Pⓐⓗ-Ⓡⓔ

store tienda (f) Tⓔⓔ-ⓔ́N-Dⓐⓗ

straight ahead derecho Dⓔ-Ⓡⓔ́-CHⓄ

strawberry fresa (f) FR(ĕ́)-S(ah)

street calle (f) K(áh)-Y(ĕ)

string cuerda (f) KW(ĕ́)R-D(ah)

subway metro (m) M(ĕ́)-TR(o)
subterráneo (m) (Spain) S(oo)B-T(ĕ)-R(áh)-N(ĕ)-(o)

sugar azúcar (f) (ah)-S(óo)-K(ah)R

suit (clothes) traje (m) TR(áh)-H(ĕ)

suitcase maleta (f) M(ah)-L(ĕ́)-T(ah)

summer verano (m) V(ĕ)-R(áh)-N(o)

sun sol (m) S(o)L

Sunday domingo (m) D(o)-M(ée)N-G(o)

sunglasses lentes de sol (f/pl) L(ĕ́)N-T(ĕ)S D(ĕ) S(o)L

suntan lotion loción bronceadora (f)
L(o)-S(ee)-(ó)N BR(o)N-S(ĕ)-(ah)-D(ó)R-(ah)

supermarket supermercado (m)
S(oo)-P(ĕ)R-M(ĕ)R-K(áh)-D(o)

surprise sorpresa (f) S(o)R-PR(ĕ́)-S(ah)

sweet dulce D(óo)L-S(ĕ)

swim (to) nadar N(ah)-D(áh)R

swimming pool piscina (f) P(ee)-S(ée)-N(ah)

synagogue sinagoga (f) S(ee)N-(ah)-G(ó)-G(ah)

T

table mesa (f)   MĒ-Sah

tampons tampones (m/pl)   Tah M-PŌ-NĒS

tape (sticky) cinta (f)   SEEN-Tah

tape recorder grabador (m)   GRah-Bah-DŌR

tax impuesto (m)   EEM-PWĒS-TO

taxi taxi (m)   Tah K-SEE

tea té (m)   TĒ

telegram telegrama (m)   TĒ-LĒ-GRah-Mah

telephone teléfono (m)   TĒ-LĒ-FO-NO

television televisión (f)   TĒ-LĒ-VEE-SEE-ŌN

temperature temperatura (f)   TĒM-PĒ-Rah-TOO-Rah

temple templo (m)   TĒM-PLO

tennis tenis (m)   TĒ-NEES

tennis court cancha de tenis (f)
    Kah N-CHah DĒ TĒ-NEES

thank you gracias   GRah-SEE-ah S

that ese (m) / esa (f)   Ē-SĒ / Ē-Sah

the el (m) / la (f) / los (m/pl) / las (f/pl)
    ĒL / Lah / LOS / Lah S

theater teatro (m)   TĒ-ah-TRO

there allí   ah-YEE

they ellos (m/pl) / ellas (f/pl) É-YOS / É-YahS

this este ÉS-Te

thread hilo (m) EE-LO

throat garganta (f) GahR-GahN-Tah

Thursday jueves (m) Hoo-É-VeS

ticket billete (m), boleto (m)
BEE-YÉ-Te / BO-LÉ-TO

tie corbata (f) KOR-Bah-Tah

time tiempo (m) TEE-ÉM-PO

tip (gratuity) propina (f) PRO-PÉE-Nah

tire llanta (f) YahN-Tah

tired cansado KahN-Sah-DO

toast pan tostado (m) PahN TO-STah-DO

tobacco tabaco (m) Tah-Bah-KO

today hoy OY

together juntos Hoo N-TOS

toilet baño (m) BahN-YO

toilet paper papel higiénico (m)
Pah-PÉL EE-HEE-É N-EE-KO

tomato tomate (m) TO-Mah-Te
jitomate (m) HEE-TO-Mah-Te

tomorrow mañana MahN-Yah-Nah

toothache dolor de dientes (m)
DO-LOB DE DEE-EN-TES

toothbrush cepillo de dientes (m)
SE-PEE-YO DE DEE-EN-TES

toothpaste pasta de dientes (f)
PAS-Tah DE DEE-EN-TES

toothpick palillo (m)   Pah-LEE-YO

tour excursión (f)   EKS-KooB-SEE-ON

tourist turista (m) (f)   Too-BEE'S-Tah

tourist office oficina de turismo (f)
O-FEE-SEE-Nah DE Too-BEEZ-MO

towel toalla (f)   TO-ah-Yah

train tren (m)   TBEN

travel agent agente de viajes (m)
ah-HEN-TE DE VEE-ah-HES

traveler's check cheque de viajero (m)
CHE-KE DE VEE-ah-HE-BO

trip viaje (m)   VEE-ah-HE

trousers pantalones (m/pl)   PahN-Tah-LO-NES

trout trucha (f)   TBoo-CHah

truth verdad (f)   VEB-DahD

Tuesday martes (m)   MahB-TES

U

umbrella paraguas (m) Pah-Rah-GWahS

understand (to) entender eN-TeN-DeR

underwear ropa interior (f) RO-Pah eN-Te-Ree-OR

United Kingdom Reino Unido (m)
   RA-NO oo-Nee-DO

United States Estados Unidos (m/pl)
   eS-Tah-DOS oo-Nee-DOS

university universidad (f) oo-Nee-VeR-See-DahD

up arriba ah-Ree-Bah

urgent urgente ooR-HeN-Te

V

vacant desocupado De-SO-Koo-Pah-DO

vacation vacaciones (f/pl) Vah-Kah-See-ON-eS

valuable precioso PRe-See-O-SO

value valor (m) Vah-LOR

vanilla vainilla (f) VI-Nee-Yah

veal carne de ternera (f)
   KahR-Ne De TeR-Ne-Rah

vegetables legumbres (f/pl) / vegetales (m/pl)
   Le-Goom-BReS / Ve-He-Tah-LeS

view vista (f) VeeS-Tah

vinegar vinagre (m) Vee-Nah-GRe

voyage viaje (m) Vee-ah-He

W

wait! ¡espérese! ĕS-PĔ-RĔ-SĔ

waiter camarero (m) Kah-Mah-RĔ-RO
mozo (m) (Spain) MO-THO

waitress camarera (f) Kah-Mah-RĔ-Rah
moza (f) (Spain) MO-THah

want (I) quiero KEE-Ĕ-RO

water agua (f) ah-GWah

we nosotros (m/pl) NO-SO-TROS

weather tiempo (m) TEE-ĔM-PO

Wednesday miércoles (m) MEE-ĔR-KO-LĔS

week semana (f) SĔ-Mah-Nah

weekend fin de semana (m) FEEN DĔ SĔ-MahN-ah

welcome ¡bienvenido! BEE-ĔN-VĔ-NEE-DO

well cooked bien cocida BEE-ĔN KO-SEE-Dah

west oeste (m) O-ĔS-TĔ

what? ¿qué? KĔ / ¿cómo? KO-MO

wheelchair silla de ruedas (f)
SEE-Yah DĔ Roo-Ĕ-DahS

when? ¿cuándo? KWahN-DO

where? ¿dónde? DON-DĔ

which? ¿cuál? KWahL

white blanco BL@N-K©

who? ¿quién? K©-©N

why? ¿por qué? P©R-K©

wife esposa (f) ©S-P©-S@h

window ventana (f) V©N-T@h-N@h

wine list lista de vinos (f) L©S-T@h D© V©-N©S

wine vino (m) V©-N©

winter invierno (m) ©N-V©-©R-N©

with con K©N

woman mujer (f) M©-H©R

wonderful maravilloso M@h-R@h-V©-Y©-S©

world mundo (m) M©N-D©

wrong equivocado / incorrecto
©-K©-V©-K@h-TH© / ©N-K©-R©K-T©

XYZ

year año (m) @N-Y©

yellow amarillo @h-M@h-R©-Y©

yes sí S©

yesterday ayer @h-Y©R

you usted (formal) ©-ST©D / tú (informal) T©

zipper cierre (m) S©-©-R©

zoo zoológico (m) S©-©-L©-H©-K©

EASILY PRONOUNCED LANGUAGE SYSTEMS

Author Clyde Peters graduated from Radford High School and the University of Hawaii and has traveled the world as a travel writer. His innovative Say It Right phrase books have revolutionized the way languages are taught and learned. Mr. Peters invented the Vowel Symbol System for easy and correct pronunciation of virtually any language. He currently continues traveling the world working on new languages and divides his spare time between Las Vegas, Nevada, and Hawaii.

Betty Chapman is a successful business woman who along with Mr. Peters founded Easily Pronounced Language Systems to promote education, travel, and custom tailored language solutions. "Moving beyond expectation to acquisition and accomplishment is possible with EPLS."

Priscilla Leal Bailey is the senior series editor for all Say It Right products and has proved indispensable in editing and implementing the EPLS Vowel Symbol System. We are forever grateful for her belief and support.

SAY IT RIGHT SERIES
Infinite Destinations
One Pronunciation System!

Audio Editions

Say It Right App on iTunes

THANKS!

The nicest thing you can say to anyone in any language is "Thank you." Try some of these languages using the incredible EPLS Vowel Symbol System.

Arabic
SH⑩-KRⓐN

Chinese
SH㊉㊉ SH㊉㉫

French
M㊉R-S㊉㊉

German
DⓐN-K⑩

Hawaiian
Mⓐ-Hⓐ-L⑩

Italian
GRⓐT-S㊉㊉-㉫

Japanese
D⑩-M⑩

Portuguese
⑩-BR㊉㊉-Gⓐ-D⑩

Russian
SPⓐ-S㊉㊉-Bⓐ

Spanish
GRⓐ-S㊉㊉-ⓐS

Swahili
ⓐ-SⓐN-T④

Tagalog
Sⓐ-Lⓐ-MⓐT

180

INDEX

QUICK REFERENCE PAGE

Hello	**Good-bye**
Hola	Adiós
O-Lah	ah-DEE-OS

How are you?	**Fine / Very well**
¿Cómo está?	Muy bien
KO-MO eS-Tah	MWEE BEE-eN

Yes	**No**
Sí	No
SEE	NO

Please	**Thank you**
Por favor	Gracias
POR Fah-FOR	GRah-SEE-ahS

I would like...	**Where is...**
Quisiera...	¿Dónde está?
KEE-SEE-e-Rah	DON-De eS-Tah...

I don't understand.

¡No entiendo!

NO eN-TEE-eN-DO

Help!

Socorro!

SO-KO-RO

182